INDIAN TOURISM
BEYOND THE MILLENNIUM

INDIAN TOURISM
BEYOND THE MILLENNIUM

M.P. Bezbaruah

GYAN PUBLISHING HOUSE
NEW DELHI-110002

Indian Tourism Beyond the Millennium
(Tourism)

ISBN : 81-212-0621-9

Second Revised and Enlarged Editon
Published in 2000 in India by
Gyan Publishing House
5, Ansari Road
New Delhi-110002

Cover Photo by Probal Sarkar
Back Cover Photo & Insides all Photos
by Phal S. Gircta, PQRS (India)

Printed by : **MEHRA OFFSET PRESS**

To

My Parents

Contents

Foreword

When I was requested by Mr Bezbaruah to write the foreword for his book entitled "Indian Tourism Beyond the Millennium", I naturally felt honoured. However, it was only until I read the book entirely that I realised what a privilege I had been given. Working in the tourism industry for as long as I have, numerous books on tourism have passed through my hands. Books on local, regional or global tourism, tourism statistics, tourism development, marketing or promotion and a score of other subjects. So the question arose—do we need another book about tourism? We could go even further. Do we need another on tourism in India? The answer, upon reading this book, was undoubtedly yes.

As the beginning of the new millennium nears, it is a very opportune moment to review the importance and impact that tourism has had on the economic, social and environmental aspects of the world. Furthermore, given the importance that tourism is projected to have in the future, it is timely to prepare well thought out strategies for the successful and sustainable development and promotion of tourism, both in the short and long term.

Mr Bezbaruah is a highly respected official in the international tourism industry. His leadership in developing and promoting tourism in India, one of the most attractive and popular tourism destinations in the world, has been appreciated ever since he took up the position as Secretary of Tourism in India in January, 1997. Mr Bezbaruah's distinguished background as Home Secretary to the Government of Assam, Minister (Economic) in the High Commission of India in London and Principal Adviser to Transport and Tourism in the Planning Commission has allowed him to play a key role in the important phase of economic reforms and liberalisation that took place in India between 1990 and 1994. He has represented India in a number of important WTO meetings and events with distinction and his contributions have been appreciated by other participants.

Tourism plays an extremely important role in the economic and social development of most countries in the world. It is the largest generator of employment and its services range from travel, accommodation, catering, maintenance of culture and traditions especially the handicraft industry, to the preservation of ecosystems. WTO forecasts that tourism arrivals and receipts worldwide will more than double by 2020. WTO's Vision 2020 document predicts that South Asia would continue to register strong growth rates and will follow the same path as South-East Asia did during the late '80s and early '90s. In the 1990s, South Asia has been the region with the highest level of growth in tourist arrivals and this has been due to the strong growth of tourism in India. India is the main South Asian tourism destination. It captures more than half of the tourist arrivals and around 75 per cent of the tourist receipts to South Asia. With this in mind, one must appreciate Mr Bezbaruah's initiative in analysing the Indian tourism sector and providing sound arguments as to the path it should take in the future.

The book is divided into seven chapters dealing with analysis of tourism on a global scale; the Indian tourism scenario; case studies of tourism development in India; public-private sector partnership; ecology and tourism; and, the future of tourism in India.

India is an extremely diverse country and tourism officials understand that there can be no single perspective of development for the entire country. The case studies presented in the book examine the role that tourism can play in the development of a more underdeveloped area as well as the need to ensure the preservation of cultural heritage.

Tourism has seen a trend over the years from being a predominantly public sector to more and more active interaction with the private sector. In a country like India where the government has so many services to provide for the people, partnerships with the private sector allow it to develop the tourism industry with a better distribution of financial responsibilities. This can prove to be a fundamental step towards the successful development of sustainable tourism in India in the future.

Given its high population, there is a strong pressure put on land availability in India. India is extremely rich in natural resources and a fine balance must be struck to ensure the longevity of the unique flora and fauna to be found there. The nature of tourists is also changing. More and more people are travelling to destinations that cater to ecotourism or to destinations that allow for minimum impact of tourism to the surroundings. Tourism development in Indian should be conducted in a way to ensure a balance between economic development of the sector and the environmental sustainability of the industry and Mr Bezbaruah presents India's policies in this regard.

Finally, Mr Bezbaruah concludes the book by presenting his views on the action to be taken in the Indian tourism industry in order to make India a top tourism destination in the world. He has realised the importance of recognising India's strengths and constraints in this regard and has thus suggested courses of actions taking these into account.

Mr Bezbaruah's experience and knowledge of tourism allow him to make very sound and practical suggestions that, if acted upon, will prove to be very useful tools for the successful development and promotion of tourism not only in India, but for tourism as a whole.

I recommend the book to academics and practitioners alike.

OMT. WTO. BTO

Francesco Frangialli
Secretary-General
World Tourism Organization

Preface

Before I joined my present official assignment two years ago, I had, like most other people, only a hazy idea about tourism as an elitist sector. Trying to promote tourism in the country I soon realised that there were big gaps in perception in many quarters. I was amazed by the complexity of all the interdependent influences that shape tourism of a country and was impressed by the vast potentials of tourism as a vehicle of socio-economic development in our country. The first task, to my mind, therefore, was to create awareness about tourism and naturally I decided to start with myself. I found my serious efforts to learn about tourism quite rewarding. At the end of the year, looking back, I found that I had spoken on tourism on numerous occasions, some of them serious, some ceremonial. Many listeners asked for more details of the statistics and ideas I used. I was convinced that there was a need to put all my thoughts expressed in these lectures in the form of a book.

I was, however, not satisfied with the results. I always had the feeling that it was not complete and many important issues were not covered. However, on introspection, I had to accept the fact that even in a life-time's work I could not hope to tackle all the diverse issues in one book.

I am grateful to Shri Madan Lal Khurana, Minister of Tourism and Parliamentary Affairs, Government of India and Shri Omak Apang, Minister of State for Tourism for so readily and graciously allowing me to use many of the government documents. I am deeply indebted to Mr Francesco Frangialli, Secretary General of World Tourism Organization, ever, so keen on development of tourism in India, who readily agreed to write the foreword to the book and also allowed free use of all WTO published materials. Dr H. Verma, Regional Representative of WTO, as always was helpful with ideas, suggestions and encouragement. I must also thank Mr G. Lipman, President, World Travel and Tourism Council for his personal interest in the book and for allowing the use of WTTC materials — from which I have drawn freely.

The cartoon drawing by Shri Sudhir Dar has enhanced the value of the book. I am grateful to him for this kind gesture and to Ms Chandni Luthra for her keen interest in the book.

I would like to sincerely thank Shri Inder Jeet Mittal without whose laborious work, the book in this present form would not have been possible. He meticulously went through the proofs, made useful suggestions and took the entire responsibility of liaison with the press.

My thanks are also due to Shri D.D. Dhingra and Shri J.P. Malhotra and all other members of my staff for helping with the typing and taking care of various miscellaneous work.

The book is a first step in the fulfilment of my promise made to my dear daughters—Supriya and Supriti— to try to make amends for my unfulfilled academic ambitions. My wife, Anuradha, cheerfully took on the onerous job of going through the first draft and by her critical comments and suggestions helped in the evolution of the book in the present form from a few disjointed lectures.

If the book can make even a small contribution towards creating awareness, I shall feel amply rewarded.

M.P. Bezbaruah

Acknowledgements

Ministry of Tourism, Government of India
for allowing the use of —

- The National Tourism Policy, 1982;
- National Action Plan, 1992; and

other published official documents.

World Tourism Organisation (WTO)
World Tourism and Travel Council (WTTC)
for allowing use of—
all their published documents.

1

Tourism : The Global Scenario

"Much have I travelled in the realms of gold,
And many goodly states and kingdoms seen;
Round many western Islands have I been..."

—John Keats
On First Looking into Chapman's Homer

As the world prepares to usher in the new millennium all those who are fortunate to be witnessing this watershed of history are seized with the excitement of new happenings. New ideas and vision, hopes and determination have generated frenzied enthusiasm in all spheres of human activities. However, some activities dominate human thinking more than others.

Information technology, for example, is one such sector. No other activity has so completely dominated human vision in recent times. It has changed man's lifestyle and has strengthened his confidence to scale such dizzy heights of achievements as were even beyond the realm of imagination earlier. As an economic activity, the information technology market in 1996 has been $ 630 billion and is expected to grow by 2000 to $ 937 billion.[1]

Yet, as an economic activity the importance of this so-called 'sun-rise' industry is only a shade of tourism, now being called the industry of the future. Quietly and imperceptibly tourism is making revolutionary impact on the world economic secnario. Throughout the 1980s, international tourism receipts grew faster than world trade.

Today, it is estimated to constitute a higher proportion of the value of world exports than all other sectors except crude petroleum and petroleum products, and is also the world's largest creator of jobs. And in the future, by 2020, when the world would be well into the new millennium, the projected annual average rate of growth of the tourism sector will be far above the maximum probable annual expansion of the world's wealth. Not surprising, therefore, that Mr Bill Gates, the Guru of IT, considers tourism as one of the three industries of the future. Coming from one who has shaped the dreams and imagination of millions in the nineties, it is a significant tribute to tourism.

The Past

Travel and tourism has been an important social activities of human beings from time immemorial. The dictionary meanings of 'tourism' and 'travel' are quite limited in scope but they bring out the basic essence of the terms. The Oxford Encyclopaedic English Dictionary, for example, defines 'travel' as 'go from one place to another, make a journey especially of some length or abroad' and the 'tourist' is defined as 'a person making a visit or tour as a holiday; a traveller, especially abroad'. A strict definition of the term for the purpose of any systematic analysis, however, is difficult because tourism is not only the world's largest industry but also the most diversified one. The World Tourism Organisation (WTO), the apex international organization for tourism has defined 'tourism', 'tourist' and 'traveller' as follows:

> "**Tourism**—The activities of persons travelling to and staying in places outside their usual environment for not more than one consecutive year for leisure, business and other purposes.
>
> **Tourist**—(Overnight visitor) Visitor staying at least one night in a collective or private accommodation in the place visited.
>
> **Traveller**—Any person on a trip between two or more locations."[2]

In the early periods of human civilization, such movements, from place to place were primarily in search of security or for gathering food or in search of more favourable places of habitation and cultivation. Such movements of groups of human beings were, therefore, largely nomadic in nature but slowly such motivations gave way to travels for trade and barter. As civilisation progressed and empires grew, wars for dominance became frequent. The need for keeping control over subjugated areas encouraged kings, emperors and conquerors to take up schemes for improvements in communication. Travels of emissaries and agents for collection of taxes or to keep the subjugated nations under control also opened up contacts between peoples and nations and established channels of understanding between different cultures. When coins in various forms came to be used for purposes of exchange, barter became unnecessary and travels became easier. Growth of civilisations and their spread beyond national boundaries, as for example, in the case of the Greek civilisation or the Roman civilisation helped the growth of common language. In such circumstances, travels became much easier and much more acceptable. It was, however, in the first period of the Reformation and the Renaissance that travels for leisure, or for acquiring more knowledge about different nations and cultures or for just adventure became a more prominent activity. Many prominent travellers, as we know, changed the complexion and the course of human history and knowledge about the wider world. The exploits and daring adventures of Marco Polo, Columbus, Vasco-de-Gama, Huen Tsang, Fa-Hien, Ibn Batuta and many such travellers and explorers added colour to the folklores and contributed to the growth of human understanding in international contexts.[3]

The Present

The development of more organised modes of travel and tourism has been a phenomenon primarily of the 20th Century. Tremendous changes in technology and improvement in modes of transport have made access to places easier. Growth in tourism infrastructure and modern inventions which have made life easier, have allowed more free time for travel and leisure and have provided the inducement to travel. All such factors have contributed greatly to the remarkable expansion of tourism in this century. The World Tourism Organization has outlined the main influences behind this significant progress of the tourism industry as shown in the chart below :

Factors Shaping the Development of Tourism

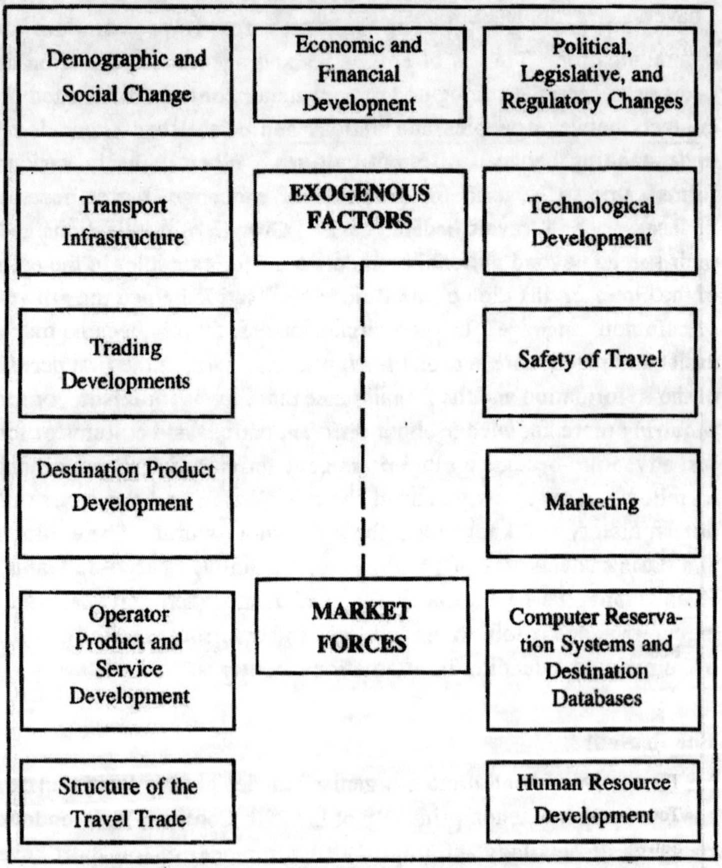

Source: World Tourism Organisation, Global Tourism Forecasts to the Year 2000 and Beyond. (Madrid: WTO, 1995), p.ix.

Not only has tourism grown, tourism has encompassed many sectors of the economy directly or indirectly making it on the one hand a very complex phenomenon and, on the other, a very important component of a country's socio-economic development strategy. It is difficult to accurately pinpoint all the activities that directly or indirectly make up the total gamut of what we call 'tourism'. It is equally difficult to identify all the direct and indirect beneficiaries of tourism. But, the following list prepared by the World Travel and Tourism Council (WTTC) may serve as a very useful benchmark of what tourism activities may encompass in any country. It is obvious that there are very few economic activities that can have a wider 'ripple' effect than tourism, because of the inter-dependence of so many small activities that make up the total picture.

The Core of the Tourism Business

Accommodation	**Hotel/Restaurant suppliers**	**Construction/Real Estate**
Hotels/Resorts		
Motels	**Taxi services**	**Distillers/Brewers/Bottlers**
Hostels		
Caravans	**Cameras and film**	**Auto/Aircraft manufacturers**
Camping		
Transportation	**Maps, travel books**	**Motor fuel producers**
Airlines		
Cruise ships	**Shopping malls**	**Clothing manufacturers**
Rail		
Car rental	**Service stations**	**Communication networks**
Bus coaches		
Attractions	**Sporting events**	**Education/training institutes**
Man-made		
Natural	**Banking services**	**Recreation/Sporting equipment**
Food and beverage		
Restaurants	**Reservation systems**	**Food producers**
Fast food		
Wine merchants	**Auto clubs**	**Advertising media**
Travel agencies		
Tour companies	**Entertainment/Art venues**	**Cartographers/Printers**
Souvenirs		
Luggage	**Museums/Historical sites**	

Source : Australian National Tourism Strategy, 1992.
Reproduced from World Travel & Tourism Council (WTTC) : Travel and Tourism : Jobs for the Millennium, 1997, p.4

The chart explains that these activities represent only the core and not the whole of tourism activities. In planning tourism development, an understanding of these activities and their inter-relationship is important. Firstly, it is evident that the activities are diverse. Their inter-relationship is in the nature of their contribution to a comprehensive tourism service. It explains both the importance of coordination and also the difficulties in achieving the same. Those who are not related to tourism and not attuned to the nuances of a sensible tourism policy, see only the parts and not the whole. Like the old story of the four blind men trying to touch and feel the elephant and getting only parts of the huge elephant and confusing them to be the whole, such confusion is ever present while talking of tourism. Secondly, the activities, as projected, highlight the role of the private sector as a driving force in tourism development and underscores the importance of partnership — a subject which we will examine at greater length later. Most of the tourism activities are driven by market forces and are influenced by the demands of the market. Yet, the Government does have an overriding role in ensuring the qualitative purity of the services and in ensuring that the market conditions function fairly.

However, the most important realisation that this chart brings out is that in our planning the frontiers of tourism activities cannot be viewed as rigid. They are ever-changing and every change encourages further refinement for higher achievements. In tourism there are infinite possibilitises of marketing the product depending on the ingenuity of the system and imagination of the human mind. What Walt Disney said in a very different context can also be applied in the case of tourism, that as long as there is any imagination left in the human mind, there will be scope for the frontiers of tourism to grow and expand.

Though the growth of tourism activities and the movement of international tourists increased substantially from the beginning of the 20th Century, the growth has been particularly rapid and noticeable in the second half of the 20th Century. Between 1950 to 1997, the international arrivals have increased from 25.3 million to 613 million whereas the receipts from tourism have increased from US $ 2.1

billion to US $ 425 billion. The following table illustrates this growth pattern.

International Tourism Activity—1950-1995*

Year	*Arrivals* (mn) *million*	*Receipts ($ billion, excluding transport)*
1950	25.3	2.1
1960	69.3	6.9
1970	165.8	17.9
1980	286.2	105.2
1990	459.2	264.7
1995	563.6	399.0
1996	595.0	425.0
Period (per cent per annum growth)	*Average Annual Percentage Increase*	*Average Annual Percentage Increase*
1950-1960	10.6	12.6
1960-1970	9.1	10.1
1970-1980	5.6	19.4
1980-1990	4.8	9.7
1990-1995	4.1	7.5
1995-1996	5.4	—

* Reproduced from *WTTC*: International Tourism. A Global Perspective, p. 18, *WTO*: Tourism Market Trends: The World, 1997.

These figures clearly illustrate the trend of growth. During the period from 1970 to 1990, the average annual growth rate reduced to about 5 per cent but this growth rate was on a sufficiently higher base that was created during the earlier two decades. During 1950 to 1970, the average annual growth in arrivals was 10 per cent. The absolute number of arrivals has almost multiplied two and a half times during 1960 and 1970 and thereafter it has almost doubled every decade. Similarly, the average annual growth rate in tourist receipts has always been much higher than the rate of growth of arrivals.

Such growth of tourism has much wider implications than just tourism earnings. The magnitude of contribution of tourism to the world economy in recent times has been equally impressive. Tourism has had more substantial contribution to the world economy than many other sectors which are normally considered to be vital for a country's growth. In 1990, as percentage of the value of world export, tourism ranked higher than electronic equipments, clothing, textiles, iron & steel and was only marginally below automobiles and crude petroleum products.

The total role of tourism in the world's economic scenario is brought out by the figures in Table 1.1.

The Table below illustrates at a glance the magnitude of contributions of tourism and its share in the world's economic activities. Some of the contributions of tourism are weighed as percentage of the total economic activities in this Table.

Share of Tourism in World Economic Activities

	1996
Jobs	255 million
Employment	1 in 9
Output	$ 3.6 trillion
per cent of GDP	10.7 per cent
Consumption	$ 2.1 trillion
per cent of total	11.3 per cent
Investment	$ 766 billion
per cent of total	11.9 per cent
Taxes	$ 653 billion
per cent of total	10.4 per cent
Exports	$ 761 billion
per cent of total	11.4 per cent

Source : *WTTC* : 1996/97 Travel and Tourism Report, p. 35.

However, the growth pattern across the countries is not evenly spread out. The ten most popular destinations in 1996 were—France, USA, Spain, Italy, UK, China, Mexico, Hungary, Poland and Canada (Table 1.2.). China and Poland have made significant progress in recent times to join the elite league at the top of the table. Among the Asian countries Indonesia, Thailand, Malaysia, Hong Kong and Singapore have shown good progress. India's position has more or less remained unchanged. However, in terms of receipts, India has a much higher position (Table 1.3).

It can also be seen from Table 1.2 that the top ten destinations account for more than half of the total tourist arrivals or of tourism receipts. The geographical spread is also uneven. Six of the top ten receiving countries are European nations.

Table 1.3 of 'tourism receipts' of the countries shows similar patterns for receipts as well. Here again, seven of the first ten are European countries and the first ten account for more than 50 per cent of the total receipts.

Tourism's significant contribution to the world economy, and in particular to production and employment, is now being increasingly recognized. Tourism can play an important role in a country's socio-economic development. The figures of tourist arrivals and earnings shown in the tables also highlight a disquieting fact that perhaps in the developing countries, which need such development thrust more than others, tourism has not yet been an important socio-economic input.

With all this growth, impressive as it is, it will only be touching the tip of actual potentials. The future annual rate of growth projected at 4.3 per cent will be far above the maximum probable expansion of 3 per cent per annum in world's wealth. In spite of such impressive figures, the World Tourism Organization has shown that if the international tourist arrivals are adjusted to the numbers of active international tourists, the proportion of world's population engaged in international tourism is only 3.5 per cent. After adjustment for those who are unable because of age, illness or financial reasons to undertake international travel, the real potential number of tourists by 2020 will only be 7 per cent. As it has been said earlier, this industry termed as "the industry of the future" is, in fact, still in its infancy.

Yet, to take advantage of the phenomenal growth, it is essential to be alive to the major determinants and influences which will shape the future. One major development which will affect many of the developing countries is spread of harmonization of currencies and political and geographical integration. Economically, in spite of the current recession and the widespread financial crisis, the future growth areas are expected to be in

Asia. Such economic growth projections, if that take shape as projected, will certainly affect both the inbound and outbound composition of tourists. Towering above all influences will be the technological developments both in information technology and transport technology. The change in demographic factors too influences the composition of the tourists by age groups. Because of such factors, the growing volumes of tourists from Europe, North America and Japan in future will be over 50 years of age.

The nature of tourism packaging will, therefore, have to be suited to the requirements of the new tourist classes. There is greater focus now on delivering unique experiences for tourists or to fashion tourism attractions tailored to the customer's tastes and demands.

Tourism primarily deals with choice of tourists, and human choices being so diverse, it is not possible to recount all the influences that may shape the pattern of tourism growth. However, recognising some of the major determinants, many countries are already fashioning their response to suit those requirements. A sample survey of 85 countries responding to WTO's Tourism 2020 Vision showed a consistency in strategic thinking on the priorities. The following areas were indentified as key priorities:

- Increased, more focused and more aggressive marketing.
- Constant striving for a competitive edge through a combination (usually of all three) of product differentiation, quality and/or price.
- Growing recognition of the need for sustainable tourism development to ensure long term prosperity.
- Less state control, and more state/private sector partnerships.[4]

What will such development imply for India? Basically, India has to position itself to get maximum benefit out of the tourism boom that is expected. To translate such intentions to actual action will imply that we need to move away from the beaten track to explore areas of our internal strength and comparative advantage in relation to our competitors. We must provide what is unique and what tourists may be willing to look for. Fortunately, our thousands of years of civilization have bestowed us with cultural traditions and variety which we can utilise to great advantage. Culture is an expression of the soul of the nation and our culture has been the culmination of expression of the richness of our lives, experiences and ideas over the years. To the outside world, India can be projected as the place where one can savour the wisdom of ages. It is also a place to experience the uplifting feeling of knowing oneself. Through the ages, millions have experienced that exhilarating feeling of going to the depth of such realisation as only the contact with a culture rich with centuries of accumulated wisdom can give. Unfortunately, sometimes we need outside agencies to tell us what those experiences are and what we have with us. We have the example of the pop group the 'Beatles' who made transcendental meditation famous.

Many recent isolated experiences in India have confirmed that we stand to gain while promoting India by emphasising the inherent strengths of our heritage and building on it. In the southern Indian State of Kerala, innovations based on traditional medicines have caught up quite well with the foreign tourists. The concept of 'The Palace on Wheels' fires the imagination of those who look for exotic experiences. The Toy Train of the eastern hill station Darjeeling, the 'Fairy Queen' of 1855 vintage steam engine etc., have been good attractions. Converting the old *havelis* (place of residence), forts and palaces strewn with history and romance into Heritage hotels has fascinated those who have the money to spend and who enjoy the out of the ordinary experience. In the vast expanse of this country are scattered innumerable such innovative potentials. These can be picked up and fitted into a marketing plan which is nurtured culturally and sensitively around the expectations of those whom we want to attract.

References

1. A.K. Chakrawarty : IT 2001 : Advantage India–Macropicture Telematics India, March, 1998.
2. *W.T.O.*: International tourism : A global perspective. ed. Chucky Y. Gee, Madrid, 1997, p. 5.
3. *W.T.O.*: *Ibid.*, p. 9.
4. W.T.O. Tourism 2020 Vision Executive Summary, June 1998. p. 35.

Table 1.1
World Estimates of Travel and Tourism 1996 (US $ billions)

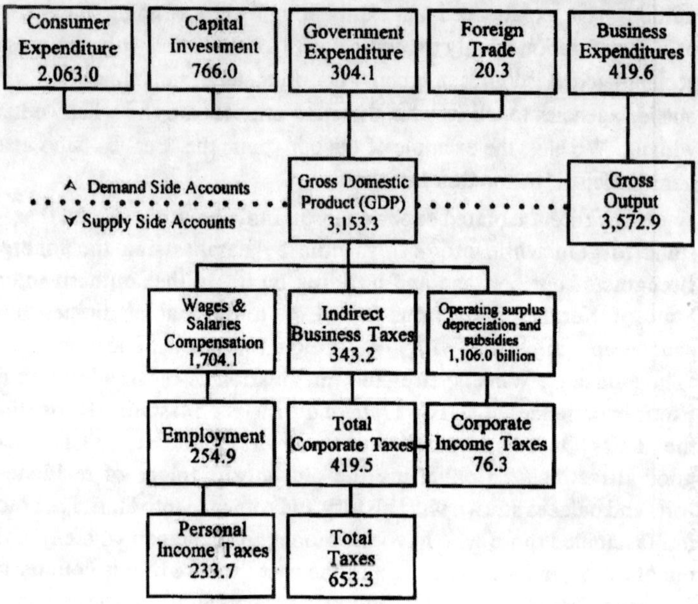

Source : 1996/97 WTTC Travel and Tourism Report, p. 11

WORLD'S TOP TOURISM DESTINATIONS

INTERNATIONAL TOURIST ARRIVALS

RANK			TOURIST ARRIVALS (THOUSAND)		AVERAGE ANNUAL GROWTH RATE (%)	% SHARE OF ARRIVALS WORLDWIDE	
1980	1997	COUNTRY	1980	1997	1980/1997	1980	1997
1	1	FRANCE	30,100	66,864	4.81	10.52	10.95
2	2	UNITED STATES	22,500	47,754	4.53	7.87	7.82
3	3	SPAIN	22,388	43,403	3.97	7.83	7.11
4	4	ITALY	22,087	34,087	2.59	7.72	5.58
7	5	UNITED KINGDOM	12,420	25,515	4.33	4.34	4.18
18	6	CHINA	3,500	23,770	11.93	1.22	3.89
13	7	POLAND	5,664	19,520	7.55	1.98	3.20
8	8	MEXICO	11,945	19,351	2.88	4.18	3.17
6	9	CANADA	12,876	17,285	1.75	4.50	2.83
10	10	HUNGARY	9,413	17,248	3.63	3.29	2.82
-	11	CZECH REPUBLIC	-	16,830	-	-	2.76
5	12	AUSTRIA	13,879	16,647	1.08	4.85	2.73
9	13	GERMANY	11,122	15,837	2.10	3.89	2.59
-	14	RUSSIAN FEDERATION	-	15,350	-	-	2.51
11	15	SWITZERLAND	8,873	10,600	1.05	3.10	1.74
28	16	CHINA, HONGKONG SAR	1,748	10,406	11.06	0.61	1.70
21	17	PORTUGAL	2,730	10,172	8.04	0.95	1.67
16	18	GREECE	4,796	10,070	4.46	1.68	1.65
52	19	TURKEY	921	9,040	14.38	0.32	1.48
27	20	THAILAND	1,859	7,221	8.31	0.65	1.18
20	21	NETHERLANDS	2,784	6,674	5.28	0.97	1.09
22	22	SINGAPORE	2,562	6,531	5.66	0.90	1.07
25	23	MALAYSIA	2,105	6,211	6.57	0.74	1.02
17	24	BELGIUM	3,777	6,037	2.80	1.32	0.99
24	25	IRELAND	2,258	5,557	5.44	0.79	0.91
55	26	SOUTH AFRICA	700	5,437	12.82	0.24	0.89
58	27	INDONESIA	527	5,185	14.40	0.18	0.85
46	28	ARGENTINA	1,120	4,540	8.58	0.39	0.74
53	29	AUSTRALIA	905	4,318	9.63	0.32	0.71

32	30	TUNISIA	1,602	4,263	5.93	0.56	0.70
37	31	JAPAN	1,317	4,218	7.09	0.46	0.69
50	32	KOREA, REPUBLIC OF	976	3,908	8.50	0.34	0.64
-	33	CROATIA	-	3,834	-	-	0.63
40	34	EGYPT	1,253	3,657	6.50	0.44	0.60
29	35	MACAU	1,656	3,610	4.69	0.58	0.59
23	36	SAUDI ARABIA	2,475	3,594	2.22	0.87	0.59
30	37	PUERTO RICO	1,639	3,249	4.11	0.57	0.53
34	38	MOROCCO	1,425	3,072	4.62	0.50	0.50
19	39	ROMANIA	3,270	2,957	-0.59	1.14	0.48
39	40	BRAZIL	1,271	2,850	4.86	0.44	0.47
41	41	NORWAY	1,252	2,702	4.63	0.44	0.44
26	42	BULGARIA	1,933	2,684	1.95	0.68	0.44
36	43	SWEDEN	1,366	2,386	3.34	0.48	0.39
44	44	INDIA	1,194	2,374	4.13	0.42	0.39
35	45	TAIWAN (Prov. of China)	1,393	2,372	3.18	0.49	0.39
48	46	URUGUAY	1,067	2,312	4.67	0.37	0.38
49	47	PHILIPPINES	1,008	2,223	4.76	0.35	0.36
67	48	DOMINICAN REPUBLIC	383	2,211	10.86	0.13	0.36
31	49	DENMARK	1,619	2,158	1.70	0.57	0.35
72	50	CYPRUS	353	2,088	11.02	0.12	0.34
47	51	ISRAEL	1,116	2,010	3.52	0.39	0.33
98	52	BAHRAIN	150	1,848	15.92	0.05	0.30
38	53	FINLAND	1,273	1,832	2.16	0.45	0.30
77	54	UNITED ARAB EMIRATES	300	1,792	11.09	0.10	0.29
-	55	VIET NAM	-	1,716	-	-	0.28
62	56	CHILE	420	1,644	8.36	0.15	0.27
45	57	BAHAMAS	1,181	1,592	1.77	0.41	0.26
57	58	COLOMBIA	553	1,544	6.23	0.19	0.25
61	59	NEW ZEALAND	465	1,497	7.12	0.16	0.25
80	60	ZIMBABWE	243	1,495	11.28	0.08	0.24
		TOTAL 1-60	249,712	567,157	4.94	87.31	92.86
		WORLD TOTAL	**285,997**	**610,763**	**4.56**	**100.00**	**100.00**

Source : World Tourism Organization (WTO)

WORLD'S TOP TOURISM EARNERS

INTERNATIONAL TOURISM RECEIPTS

RANK			TOURIST RECEIPTS (US $ MILLION)		AVERAGE ANNUAL GROWTH RATE (%)	% SHARE OF RECEIPTS WORLDWIDE	
1980	1997	COUNTRY	1980	1997	1980/1997	1980	1997
1	1	UNITED STATES	10,058	73,268	12.39	9.55	16.81
3	2	ITALY	8,213	29,714	7.86	7.80	6.82
2	3	FRANCE	8,235	28,009	7.47	7.82	6.42
4	4	SPAIN	6,968	26,651	8.21	6.62	6.11
5	5	UNITED KINGDOM	6,932	20,039	6.44	6.58	4.60
6	6	GERMANY	6,566	16,509	5.57	6.23	3.79
7	7	AUSTRIA	6,442	12,393	3.92	6.12	2.84
34	8	CHINA	617	12,074	19.12	0.59	2.77
19	9	CHINA, HONG KONG SAR	1,317	9,242	12.14	1.25	2.12
24	10	AUSTRALIA	967	9,026	14.04	0.92	2.07
10	11	CANADA	2,284	8,770	8.24	2.17	2.01
51	12	POLAND	282	8,679	22.33	0.27	1.99
46	13	TURKEY	327	8,088	20.77	0.31	1.86
9	14	SWITZERLAND	3,149	7,902	5.56	2.99	1.81
8	15	MEXICO	5,393	7,594	- (1)	5.12	1.74
27	16	THAILAND	867	7,048	13.12	0.82	1.62
-	17	RUSSIAN FEDERATION	-	6,900	-	-	1.58
16	18	SINGAPORE	1,433	6,843	9.63	1.36	1.57
15	19	NETHERLANDS	1,668	6,219	8.05	1.58	1.43
56	20	INDONESIA	246	5,437	19.97	0.23	1.25
12	21	BELGIUM	1,810	5,275	6.49	1.72	1.21
41	22	KOREA, REPUBLIC OF	369	5,116	16.73	0.35	1.17
43	23	ARGENTINA	345	5,069	17.13	0.33	1.16
32	24	JAPAN	644	4,326	11.86	0.61	0.99
21	25	PORTUGAL	1,147	4,277	8.05	1.09	0.98
14	26	GREECE	1,734	3,771	4.68	1.65	0.86
28	27	EGYPT	808	3,727	9.41	0.77	0.85
-	28	CZECH REPUBLIC	-	3,647	-	-	0.84
25	29	SWEDEN	962	3,572	8.02	0.91	0.82

23	30	TAIWAN (Prov. of China)	988	3,402	7.54	0.94	0.78
37	31	IRELAND	472	3,189	11.89	0.45	0.73
18	32	DENMARK	1,337	3,156	5.18	1.27	0.72
20	33	INDIA	1,150	3,152	6.11	1.09	0.72
-	34	MACAU	-	2,947	-	-	0.68
48	35	PHILIPPINES	320	2,831	13.68	0.30	0.65
26	36	ISRAEL	903	2,741	6.75	0.86	0.63
52	37	MALAYSIA	265	2,703	14.64	0.25	0.62
13	38	BRAZIL	1,794	2,595	2.20	1.70	0.60
69	39	HUNGARY	160	2,582	17.77	0.15	0.59
-	40	CROATIA	-	2,529	-	-	0.58
31	41	SOUTH AFRICA	652	2,297	7.69	0.62	0.53
29	42	NORWAY	751	2,226	6.60	0.71	0.51
66	43	DOMINICAN REPUBLIC	168	2,107	16.04	0.16	0.48
60	44	NEW ZEALAND	211	2,093	14.45	0.20	0.48
33	45	PUERTO RICO	619	2,046	7.29	0.59	0.47
30	46	FINLAND	677	1,963	6.46	0.64	0.45
62	47	CYPRUS	203	1,639	13.07	0.19	0.38
64	48	GUAM	179	1,450	13.09	0.17	0.33
39	49	MOROCCO	397	1,443	7.89	0.38	0.33
35	50	TUNISIA	601	1,423	5.20	0.57	0.33
17	51	SAUDI ARABIA	1,344	1,420	0.32	1.28	0.33
36	52	BAHAMAS	596	1,416	5.22	0.57	0.32
100	53	CUBA	40	1,338	22.93	0.04	0.31
-	54	SLOVENIA	-	1,188	-	-	0.27
58	55	JAMAICA	242	1,131	9.49	0.23	0.26
57	56	VENEZUELA	243	1,086	9.21	0.23	0.25
70	57	SYRIAN ARAB REPUBLIC	156	1,035	11.77	0.15	0.24
68	58	CHILE	166	1,021	11.28	0.16	0.23
-	59	LEBANON	-	1,000	-	-	0.23
42	60	COLOMBIA	357	955	5.96	0.34	0.22
		TOTAL 1-60	94,774	411,289	9.02	89.99	94.34
		WORLD TOTAL	**105,320**	**435,981**	**8.72**	**100.00**	**100.00**

(1) Data for 1980 not comparable with data for 1997 due to change of series.
Source : World Tourism Organization (WTO)

2

India–Looking Back

"On the verandah of the Cecil Hotel
Miss Penelope (canary colored hair,
woollen stockings and walking stick) has been saying
for thirty years: Oh India,
Country of missed opportunities..."

— Octavio Paz, 'Ootacamand'
The Collected Poems, 1988

Travel and tourism in India is an integral part of Indian tradition and culture. In the olden days, travel was primarily for pilgrimage–as the holy places dotting the countryside attracted people from different parts of the vast sub-continent. People also travelled to participate in melas, fairs and festivals in different parts of the country. In such a background developed a cultural tradition where ***'Atithi Devo Bhava'*** (the guest is god) and ***'Vasudhaiva Kutumbakam'*** (the world is one family) became bywords of Indian social behaviour. From ancient time , the rulers in different parts of India built luxurious palaces, enchanting gardens, marvellous temples, grand forts, tombs and memorials giving expression to the depth of one's feelings and sentiments. These remain today as testimony to the rich cultural heritage of this land, and as examples of exquisite craftsmanship of the people of the ages gone past. The variety of such creation is exciting. The grandeur of many of these is quite breathtaking. The beauty of India's cultural heritage and the richness of nature's endowments, make India a tourists' paradise. The words of the famous Orientalist, Max Mueller aptly sum up the strength of India : "If we were to look over the whole world to find out the country most richly endowed with all the wealth, power and beauty that nature can bestow — in some parts a veritable paradise on earth—I should point to India. If I were asked under what sky the human mind has most fully developed some of its choicest gifts... I should point to India."[1]

The dimensions of tourism changed as trade and commerce developed. The spice trade brought India into contact with the world more than before. The silk route trade also opened up India's immense cultural heritage and natural beauty to the world outside. The establishment of the Indian Railways by the British, modernisation of the ports, development of hill stations — all these added to the growth of the Indian tourism industry in the 19th and the early part of the 20th century.

The growth of modern, organised tourism, however, was slow. Systematic information, even if inadequate, has been available only during the post-Independence era. It was only after the '80s that tourism as an industry picked up speed.

In 1982, the first National Tourism Policy was formulated. Till then, the importance of tourism for earning foreign exchange was being increasingly recognised. Yet for thirty five years after Independence, there was no consensus even on the need to have a long-term consistent tourism policy.

Mr Som Nath Chib, the first Director General of Tourism of India, in his Patel Memorial Lecture in 1981 relates the debate that was going on about the need for a policy.

"Apropos a tourism policy it would be pertinent to mention that the Estimates Committee of Parliament in their 42nd Report of 1972-73 recommended that :

> 'Government should formulate a tourist promotion policy and bring it forward as a Resolution so that the policy in this behalf is put on a stable and assured basis.'

The Government's reply in Parliament was:

> "The national policy on tourism has already been laid down from time to time in successive plans which provide a clear framework for implementation at all levels. In this connection it has to be borne in mind that tourism is a fast changing activity and Government has to keep its options open to adjust its policies and programmes according to the changing needs of international tourism."

It would be difficult to accept the argument that successive Five Year Plans are a substitute for a national policy on tourism, or that because tourism was a fast changing activity, a national policy would bind the Government to certain objectives and thus would come in the way of making adjustments according to the changing needs of international tourism. Not surprisingly, the Estimates Committee did not accept this plea and again in 1975 asked the Government to indicate clearly whether it intended to formulate any definitive tourism policy or not. The Secretary, Ministry of Tourism and Civil Aviation, while testifying before the Committee, admitted that: "The fact is that there has been no formal formulation of tourism policy in the sense that you are wanting". Expressing his personal view the Secretary said, "The objective of the tourism policy of the Central Government is promotion of international tourism and to earn as much foreign exchange for the country, as is possible. This is in the context of the continuing difficulty which the country has been facing in regard to the balance of payments which, as we are all aware, has got extremely accentuated in recent times. The tourism industry is viewed by the Central Government as an export promotion effort."

The Estimates Committee thereupon reiterated its view in 1976 as follows:

"That a formal formulation of the Tourism Policy laying down the basic approach to the promotion of tourism in the country would not only reinvigorate the tourism promotion effort but would also provide a clear framework for implementation at all levels."[2]

Tourism Since Independence

Pandit Jawaharlal Nehru's oft-quoted remark : "Welcome a Tourist and send back a Friend" was the essence of India's tourism approach in the post-Independence era. Tourism was seen as an important instrument for national integration and international understanding. This was a period when the horrors of the Second World War were still fresh in memory. This was also a period of the emergence of the newly independent nations trying to forge a unity of political philosophy for a world of peaceful co-existence. The traditional role of tourism in promoting mutual understanding, was, therefore, naturally in focus. Even the Policy of 1982 states that the objective of Government is to so develop tourism that "it becomes a unifying force nationally and internationally, fostering better understanding through travel."

Whatever may be the objectives of tourism, even in those initial years of economic planning, the importance of creating the infrastructure was recognised. A full-fledged Cabinet Minister was appointed to head the Department of Tourism, and tourism development became closely linked, as it should be, to the spread of civil aviation. The Five-Star hotel Ashok, the pride of the Government in those days, came up in the' 50s. The India Tourism Development Corporation (ITDC) was set up as an umbrella organization to develop tourism infrastructure at a time when private initiative in these areas was not so abundant. Air-India too, started a Tourism Cell way back in the 1950s. These were good beginnings which indicated a certain sense of purpose.

In the global scenario, as we have seen, during the last 50 years, international tourist arrivals have increased from only 25 million in 1950 to 613 million in 1997. Tourism receipts have increased from US $ 2.1 billion to US $ 444 billion. The future projections, as already pointed out, are very impressive.

Where is Indian tourism today in this scenario? With 2.37 million foreign tourist arrivals bringing in foreign exchange receipts of approximately Rs. 11,000 crores, tourism is the second largest net foreign exchange earner in the country. The progress in arrivals and earnings since 1970 is shown in Tables 2.1 and 2.2.

But a sense of satisfaction about our progress also invariably brings up the nagging question as to why India, endowed with such varied natural beauty, cultural heritage and wide variety of tourist products, has not been able to attract tourists to the extent that many other countries, including its smaller, far less endowed neighbours in South-East Asia have been able to do? While we have made some progress and can feel happy about having a share of 51per cent of the tourist arrivals and 76.57 per cent of the tourism receipts of South Asia as a whole, there is no doubt that others around us have made greater progress and have overtaken us. On the positive side, as per the World Tourism Organization (WTO) Report, the South Asia region is projected to grow in the future at a rate of 6.1per cent, which is higher than the rate of growth for the world as a whole. However, it still leaves South Asia's present share at 0.7 per cent only and that of India's at a meagre 0.4 per cent of the total world arrivals–a very low share considering India's great potentials. As other nations have made greater progress, in the global scenario, India's ranking as a tourist destination has recently gone further down. From a position of 46 in 1985, in 1990, India showing a positive improvement, had moved up to 42. By 1996, India was down again by another rank to 43, not so much because India performed badly compared to earlier years but because others performed much better to overtake us. In terms of earnings as well, during the same period, India's position has changed from 32 to 34.

It would be fair, however, to look at both sides of the coin. Tourism development during the last 50 years certainly shows a few positive aspects.

In the first place the progress from 17,000 tourist arrivals and Rs. 7.7 crore in foreign exchange earnings in 1950 to the present arrival of 2.37 million and Rs.11,000 crores in foreign exchange earnings, is certainly an impressive one. It would, therefore, be factually incorrect to imply that we have not made any progress in tourism.

Similarly, the proportion of foreign exchange earnings to arrivals (about US $ 3 billion from 2.37 million arrivals) is higher compared to most of the top tourist arrival countries. In 1996, China, for example, with 26 million arrivals, showed an earning of US $ 10 billion only.

Moreover, to have a correct perspective of tourism development, it is necessary to take a comprehensive view of tourism and not just a fragmented one in terms of foreign tourist arrivals only. Domestic tourism promotion has been the foundation of Indian tourism policy right from the beginning. This sector has shown a phenomenal growth, reaching a figure of about 140 million in 1997. Added to that are about 100 million religious tourists who do not come within the normal statistical parameters. These domestic tourists utilise the same infrastructure and enjoy the same tourism products that the foreign tourists do. The State governments have the primary responsibility for making such domestic tourism possible and for promoting it. Over the years, substantial progress has been made in developing the required infrastructure that has made such a growth in domestic tourism possible. It is a different matter that the infrastructure available is inadequate to meet the growing tourism needs, or that there is much scope for qualitative improvement. But, no objective analysis can overlook the progress made so far.

The overall impact of tourism on India's economy has also been significant. In 1995, apart from 9.1 million direct employment and estimated 12.3 million indirect employment, tourism receipts were 0.9 per cent of Gross National Product (GNP), 9.0 per cent of merchandise export and 56 per cent of commercial services export.[3]

One has also to appreciate that it is illogical to compare the incomparables. Many countries that are compared with India, differ in fundamentals, e.g. in the form and content of Governments, size of the country, the moral and ethical values of society. Such, and many other parameters make all the difference.

Yet, such arguments to emphasise the positive aspects of tourism development in the country will appear to be a tediously pedantic exercise unless they are seen in the context of the ground realities that guide tourism in India. Such arguments cannot conceal the undeniable realities that Indian achievement is way behind its actual capabilities and potentials and, that tourism has not been able to play its role as an important instrument of socio-economic development. To find an answer to the question as to why it has not, one has to look at the constraints which inhibit such achievements. If India is to achieve a much higher growth in tourism in the years to come, and make up for the lost time, greater emphasis will have to be placed on removing these constraints to growth of tourism. The first step in such an effort will have to be to create an atmosphere congenial to the development of tourism, to spread awareness about the importance of tourism, to prepare the nation to partake of the great world tourism boom and in short, to create a culture of tourism. It will be pertinent, therefore, at this stage to make an assessment of the nation's perception about tourism as reflected in the Government policy papers like the Five Year Plan documents and the National Tourism Policy, 1982.

Tourism in the Five Year Plans

The Five Year Plan is like a mirror of the country's perception about the directions of socio-economic progress. Therefore, it is useful to have a look at the perception of the national policy planners on tourism as reflected in the Five Year Plans of the country. The allocations for tourism from the First Plan onwards and the percentage allocation for tourism in relation to the total plan outlay is as depicted in the following Tables :—

I.	*Five Year Plans*	*Tourism (Rs. in crore)*	*Percentage of total Plan outlay*
	First Plan	Not mentioned	-
	Second Plan	Not mentioned	-
	Third Plan	4.001(approx)	0.11
	Fourth Plan	25.00	0.30
	Fifth Plan	23.62	0.121
	Sixth Plan	72.00	0.15
	Seventh Plan	138.68	0.15
	Eighth Plan	272.00	0.11

II.	*Annual Plans*	*Tourism (Rs. in crore)*	*Percentage of total Plan outlay*
	1990-91	83.00	0.21
	1991-92	90.00	0.21
	1992-93	81.00	0.17
	1993-94	87.20	0.14
	1994-95	103.51	0.13
	1995-96	102.70	0.13
	1996-97	130.00	0.17
	1997-98	180.35	0.20

Source : Five Year Plan documents–Planning Commission of India.

Note : Outlay includes Budgetary Support (BS) plus Internal Extra Budgetary Resources (IEBR).

In the First Plan, there is no allocation for tourism nor is there any mention in the document about tourism. The Second Plan refers to tourism but only in relation to a few schemes. The schemes are of two categories, namely, —

(a) schemes for the development of facilities at a limited number of places visited largely by foreign tourists; and

(b) schemes intended primarily to provide facilities for home tourists of low and middle-income groups at a number of places of regional and local importance.[4]

There is no specific and separate allocation for tourism in the Second Plan.

The Third Plan, mentions that "tourism has assumed increasing importance during recent years."[5] The Third Plan programmes concentrate largely on the provision of facilities for accommodation and transport. The Plan document also makes an important distinction between Central and State schemes. While schemes in the Central sector provide for facilities which are important from the point of view of foreign tourism, those in the State Plans are intended mainly for home tourism. This emphasis on development of infrastrucutre and the distinction between the Central and the State budgets implicit in the Third Plan has been continued in the Fourth Plan as well. The Fourth Plan looks at foreign exchange earnings as the prime objective of tourism development while employment generation is also considered as an additional benefit. It states "Tourism is an important means of earning foreign exchange. It also provides employment and promotes international contacts and understanding."[6] The concept of selective approach to development of infrastructure that was to become the cornerstone of subsequent tourism policy, is mooted in the Fourth Plan, which states that "efforts will be concentrated in areas where there is an identified large flow of foreign tourist traffic."[7]

Tourism seems to have suffered a setback in emphasis, both in respect of resource allocations as well as in terms of broad objectives in the Fifth Plan. The write-up on tourism in this Plan is confined to a few programmes and financial allocations. There is no broad strategy, no perspective plan in respect of the future, and no indication about Government thinking on the issue. However, this setback is more than compensated by the Sixth Plan which perhaps marks the beginning of a new thinking on tourism in India. The emphasis also shifts from schemes to strategies and from foreign exchange earnings to wider issues of economic development. The Plan document refers to —

(a) social and economic benefits like promotion of national integration and international understanding;

(b) creation of employment;

(c) removal of regional imbalances;

(d) opening up of new growth centres in the interiors of the country;

(e) augmentation of foreign exchange earnings;

(f) support to local handicrafts and cultural activities;

(g) source of tax revenues for Government—both Central and State.[8]

While outlining the benefits of tourism, the Sixth Plan also draws attention to a very important aspect of tourism—"It is also relevant that the various multi-faceted socio-economic benefits of tourism are achieved with a relatively low level of investment."[9] Infrastructure development for tourism promotion continues to be the primary focus of attention in this Plan and the importance of environmental surroundings, preservation of local culture, etc., are duly recognized. For the first time, the concept of 'selective travel circuits' to maximise returns on investment and to obtain the most cost-efficient use of scarce resources is clearly mentioned as a strategy. The Plan document also refers to the importance of coordination of activities among the Centre, the States and the private sector, and thus brings into focus an area critical to the development of tourism. The allocation for tourism is also substantially increased. In terms of percentage of total allocation, however, it remains almost at the same level as it was for the Fifth Plan.

The Seventh Plan includes a refreshingly clear enunciation of the role of tourism and a review of the development of tourism in India. It also sets the objectives for tourism sector as follows —

"(i) faster development of tourism;

(ii) according the status of an industry to tourism;

(iii) re-defining of the role of public and private sectors to ensure that the private sector investment is encouraged in developing tourism and the public sector investment is focussed mainly on development of support infrastructure; and

(iv) exploiting tourism potential to support local handicrafts and other creative arts and to promote national integration."[10]

Within these broad objectives, the Seventh Plan has also identified some thrust areas for action. Some such identified areas are :

(a) Development of tourist circuits.

(b) Diversification of tourism products and expanding the base from cultural tourism to other forms of holiday tourism.

(c) Development of non-traditional areas such as trekking, winter sports, wild life tourism, beach resort, etc.

(d) Restoration and balanced development of national Heritage products.

(e) Exploration of new tourism related markets.

(f) Launching of a National Image Building and Marketing Plan in key markets jointly with the private sector.

These are pathbreaking ideas but many of them remain to be implemented. These ideas are, therefore, still relevant for policy formulation.

The Seventh Plan is also similarly innovative in its approach to the role of the private sector and in recognizing that the private sector should be encouraged to provide infrastructural facilities.

The Eighth Plan refers to the Seventh Plan as a "watershed in the development of tourism in the country". But, in many ways, the Eighth Plan is equally significant, formulated as it was in the background of India's new economic liberalisation strategies. Interestingly, the future perspective that is outlined in the Eighth Plan is based on a presumption which itself can be debatable. It says "in the development of tourism, the public sector has made significant contributions during the last three decades. The industry is today equipped with reasonable infrastructural base and is poised for a self-sustained growth."[11] As the industry even today is awfully short of infrastructure, the picture could have been only far less promising during the Eighth Plan. To conceive of the industry as being poised for self-sustained growth, must have been, one can say with the benefit of hindsight, a very optimistic presumption or a mistaken notion.

The Eighth Plan document, however, makes a few very significant and valid observations about the future strategies. The issues identified can be summed up as follows :

(a) The future growth of tourism should be achieved mainly through private initiative.

(b) The State should confine its role to planning broad strategies of development, providing fiscal and monetary incentives to create a dynamic private sector and devising regulatory and supervisory mechanism.

(c) The strategy for development must be based on cost efficiency, higher productivity, efficiency and quality in provision of infrastructure.

(d) In view of the fact that capital is scarce, a selective approach, as was identified in the earlier Plans, should be adopted for the development of tourism. The Eighth Plan introduces the concept of 'Special Tourism Areas' — areas which will be provided full-fledged infrastructural facilities.

(e) Tourism marketing and publicity should be properly focussed, strengthened and should be "dynamic in terms of spread, innovation, imagination, new techniques and coordination". [12]

(f) Access to information and proper use of information technologies should be the basis for future development.

(g) Tourism development programmes for backward areas should be integrated with area development programmes.

(h) To achieve a balanced infrastructural development, all the States should be encouraged to formulate Master Plans.

(i) Human resource development should be of vital importance for the development of tourism.

The Eighth Plan also recognises the importance of communication in its entirety, including civil aviation, rail and road transport for the development of tourism. The Plan document, therefore, refers to the steps that are required to be taken in these sectors in coordination with tourism. Keeping in tune with the priority given to the private sector participation in the Eighth Plan, the Plan document envisages that in all the areas related to infrastructure development for tourism, private initiatives would be encouraged.

In a sense, for the first time since the beginning of India's planned economic development, the Eighth Plan provides a comprehensive review of the basic issues which need attention for the future development of tourism. These strategic perceptions are valid even in the present context when the country is already into what should have seen the second year of the 9th Plan. Perhaps because the issues and the strategies are already so clearly outlined in the Eighth Plan, the Draft Ninth Plan does not repeat the strategic options and only reiterates the Government's intention to carry forward the development of tourism in the directions already identified.

The Ninth Plan policy framework on tourism, however, introduces a few new elements of policy. First, it emphasises the importance of looking at infrastructure development for domestic tourism and, therefore, the role played by the respective States. It also elaborates on the need for effective coordination of all the relevant agencies involved in the development of proper infrastructure and in the development of the tourism products. The Ninth Plan also brings out the importance of people's participation at the grass root level for development of tourist facilities, and for creating a tourist-friendly atmosphere. Keeping in tune with the overall government policy of balanced development, the plan for tourism also makes a special reference to regional development and, in particular, to the special measures to be undertaken for development of the North-East region of India.

Today, 50 years after the country started on the road of planned economic development, tourism finds an important place in the overall strategy. It has been a slow process and often the boundaries of action on tourism were limited by an ad hoc approach. Moreover, though the Plans have covered a comprehensive area and have outlined almost all the issues relevant for the development of tourism, a clear idea about the role of tourism and its place in the overall economic development planning of the country has not yet emerged. What the Five Year Plans have achieved through the categorisation of schemes and of development programmes, is, primarily a sectoral growth strategy for tourism but not a role for tourism as a catalyst for growth. Any future vision for tourism should, therefore, be built on an integration of the strategy for the development of tourism to the basic development strategies of the country. An essential part of such a strategy, would be the coordination of the development plans of infrastructure sectors with the initiatives for promotion of tourism.

The National Tourism Policy, 1982

Long after Pandit Jawaharlal Nehru had spoken about the role of tourism in the initial years of Indian economic planning, in 1982, India formulated its one and only 'National Policy' on tourism *(Appendix-I)*. Pandit Nehru had realised the economic potentials of tourism. But, he was also a visionary trying to carve out a role for India in the assembly of newly emerging nations, for international peace and understanding. He, therefore, saw the primary role of tourism as one of fostering mutual understanding and international goodwill. The Preface to the Report of the National Committee on Tourism itself quotes Nehru, "We must welcome visitors from abroad for economic reasons, for tourism brings foreign exchange, but even more so because this leads to greater understanding and mutual appreciation. There is nothing that the world needs today more than mutual understanding."[13]

The 1982 Policy continues with this vision. It is a very important document about the nation's perception on tourism. The objective of the Policy is to so develop tourism that it —

(i) becomes a unifying force nationally and internationally fostering a better understanding;

(ii) helps preserving Indian heritage and culture and projecting the same to the world;

(iii) brings socio-economic benefits in terms of employment, income generation, revenue generation, foreign exchange, etc.;

(iv) gives direction and opportunity to the youth of the country to understand the aspirations and viewpoint of others and help in greater national integration;

(v) offers opportunities to the youth of the country, not only for employment but also for taking up activities for nation-building and character-building like sports, adventure, etc.[14]

The Policy very rightly puts emphasis on the development of domestic tourism as a foundation for future strategy. Tourism again being a multi-faceted endeavour, the government has to play the role of a catalyst. The National Policy highlights the need for coordination and appropriately refers to tourism as a 'common endeavour'. The Policy was also framed at a time when India was assessing its role in the newly emerging regional political identities. Thus, the concern for regional endeavour is reflected in the Policy which makes a direct reference to regional cooperation for tourism development in the South-Asian region. While the basic problems of tourism development have been identified in the Policy, the underlying emphasis is on national understanding and international cooperation through tourism. Even the plan of action outlined in the Policy on Tourism emphasises the importance of involving the youth of the country in national integration and of making tourism a vehicle for achieving this objective. Social and cultural contribution of tourism dominates the plan of action which talks about 'a new ethos and value to tourism'.

Expectedly, the Policy framework is in tune with the strategy outlined in the Five Year Plans. It talks about a 'selective approach', a dynamic marketing strategy, appropriate manpower development, fiscal and other incentives to be extended to the private sector and the need for a balanced development of tourism consistent with ecological and environmental considerations.

A National Committee on Tourism which was constituted soon after, submitted its Report in 1988. It is perhaps one of the most comprehensive reports on tourism development in India. Sadly, it is also a Report which has been least acted upon. Many of the observations and recommendations contained in the Report have by now flowered into piece meal policy actions but over the period no comprehensive and conscious efforts to tackle the issues raised are evident.

The preface to the Report of the National Committee on Tourism quotes Nehru's perception about the role of tourism in international understanding. The Report thus carries forward the underlying thread of the 1982 Policy. The Report had a vision for the future and the preface itself clearly outlines the fundamental issue : "the need for a national consensus on the role and level of tourism development in the country". After 10 years of the presentation this Report, as the country prepares to move into the new millennium, such a consensus is yet to emerge as an operational agenda for the government.

The Report covers all the important issues relating to the role of tourism, the need for infrastructure development, strategy of development, etc. The National Committee also made a large number of recommendations, some of which were for immediate operation, and the rest requiring long-term policy decisions. Most of these recommendations require comprehensive action programme. Some of the crucial recommendations in the Report which are still being debated are —

(1) The need for re-arranging the existing organisational structure of the Department of Tourism and the need for an apex body called the National Tourism Board.

(2) The setting up of a Standing Committee of Tourism Ministers for an integrated approach to tourism development and also to effectively associate the State Governments.

(3) To ensure implementation of the recommendations a National Policy needs to be evolved, supported by a comprehensive legislation.

(4) Tourism Plans to be integrated into overall plans of the country and into Area Development Plans.[15]

These recommendations are fundamental to any substantial tourism development strategy for the country. In a country which has such tremendous potentials for tourism development, the fact that these far-reaching recommendations are still being discussed, and debated is not a happy reflection of national consensus. Ten years after they were put forward to the government, many of the recommendations are yet to be implemented.

The National Action Plan, 1992

Logically, the National Action Plan which was drawn up in 1992 should have been an attempt to translate these ideas into action. However, the National Action Plan was only a 'plan of action' for immediate purpose and did not try to change the existing framework or to tackle the fundamental issues which require long-term-policy changes. The National Action Plan is, therefore, to be regarded as an emergency action plan to set things right in some key areas, and to provide directions of national action to achieve quick results. The objectives set out rightly focus on the perceived inadequacies of the system and incorporate all those areas which have been identified as the weaknesses of India's tourism development policy. In an important statement, the Action Plan quantifies the target of the number of international tourist arrivals to India *(Appendix-II)*.

> "Presently the foreign tourist arrivals in India constitute only about 0.4 per cent of the total foreign tourists movement all over the world. One of the objectives of the Action Plan would be to increase India's share to 1 per cent within the next five years."[16]

This should have meant that steps were to be taken to more than double the international arrivals by 1997. The international tourist arrivals in 1997 was 613 million, 1 per cent of this would, in fact, be 6 million. As is well known, the country is still far away from that target.

The strategies outlined in the Action Plan for achieving these objectives are:

- "Improvement of tourism infrastructure.
- Developing areas on a selective basis for integrated growth along with marketing of destinations to ensure optimal use of existing infrastructure.
- Restructuring and strengthening the institutions for development of human resources.
- Evolving a suitable policy for increasing foreign tourist arrivals and foreign exchange earnings."[17]

The National Action Plan formally endorsed the idea of a 'Special Tourism Area' (STA) as a government strategy. Perhaps the idea of (STA) flows from the experience of Mexico where CANCUN area development programme was a great success. A study of the CANCUN experience, however, shows that it required not only a national agenda but also integration of many different activities like credit flows and financial incentives for the emergence of private initiative and regulated growth of the infrastructure. All these activities were professionally managed in a manner which is not visible in the Indian policies. The National Action Plan is non-explicit in details about the action required to be taken to achieve such an integration of activities. CANCUN was Mexico's national agenda. Mr Savignac, former Secretary General of WTO and also former Minister of Planning and Finance in Mexico, explains how such coordination was achieved.

Mexico realized that all efforts and innovative ideas ultimately boiled down to availability of resources. Departments guard their budget allocations as exclusive preserve and are generally allergic to any outside intrusion, even if such coordination is desirable from the national point of view. Realising this sensitivity, the Government of Mexico hit upon the novel idea of providing incentives to various departments to achieve the required coordination for tourism promotion. A separate government organisation was set up — known as FONATUR — National Fund for the Promotion of Tourism. Savignac beautifully explains how coordination was achieved :

> "The coordination with the various Government Ministries and Departments charged with the specific responsibility of building airports, putting in water and sewerage, telephones, electricity and other infrastructure, with ups and downs and some delays, generally went well and accomplished their jobs. Why and how you ask? Simple: the coordination was achieved by the source of the funding. The funds, allocated for each specific program by the Planning Ministry, and authorized and disbursed by the Ministry of Finance, upon the recommendation of FONATUR, were in addition to each executing Ministry's own programe and budget. No skin off their nose, so to speak, and an additional budget as a feather in their cap, so why would they not cooperate? Local, state and municipal governments happily joined in since it meant a major Central Government investment to create jobs and new sources of wealth in their areas."[18]

Tourism in India is nowhere near being accorded such a status. The National Action Plan also mentions areas of action which are important for tourism development but which fall under the control of different Ministries of the Government of India like improvement in facilities at international airports, liberalised charter flights and open sky policy for routes on which Air-India does not operate or operates in a limited fashion. These are important issues and most of them still remain to be resolved. These can be tackled effectively only when the strategy of 'common endeavour' outlined in the 1982 Policy becomes a reality.

References

1. (Max Mueller, in his lecture in Cambridge University, UK, 1882. Quoted by Jawaharlal Nehru—'The Discovery of India'. The Signet Press, Calcutta 1946, p. 90).
2. S.N. Chib: Essays on Tourism, Ed. by Ratna Sahai, Cross Section Publications Private Limited, New Delhi, 1989. p. 28-29.
3. WTO: Tourism Market Trends. The World 1997, p.128.
4. The Second Five Year Plan: Planning Commission of India, p. 480
5. The Third Five Year Plan: Planning Commission of India, p. 565
6. The Fourth Five Year Plan: Planning Commission of India, p.186
7. *Ibid.*, p. 186.
8. The Sixth Five Year Plan: Planning Commission of India, p. 309.
9. *Ibid.*, p. 309.
10. The Seventh Five Year Plan: Planning Commission of India, p. 234.
11. The Eighth Five Year Plan: Planning Commission of India, pp. 253-54.
12. *Ibid.*, p. 254.
13. Planning Commission of India: Report of the National Committee on Tourism–Preface, New Delhi, May, 1988.
14. Ministry of Tourism: Government of India–Tourism Policy (Presented by the Minister for Tourism in the both Houses of Parliament, namely, the *Lok Sabha* and the *Rajya Sabha* on November 3, 1982), p. 4.
15. Planning Commission of India–Report of the National Committee on Tourism, pp.141-44.
16. Government of India, Ministry of Civil Aviation and Tourism – National Action Plan for Tourism, p. 5, May, 1992.
17. *Ibid.*, p. 6.
18. Mr Antonio Enriquez Savignac : Foundation Day Lecture, 1997, New Delhi.

Table 2.1

Estimates of Foreign Exchange Earnings from Tourism since 1970-71

Year	*Estimated (Rs. in crores)*	*Percentage Change*
1970-71	32.5	2.2
1975-76	189.6	101.7
1980-81	1,116.3	26.8
1981-82	1,063.9	(-)8.8
1982-83	1,130.6	6.3
1983-84	1,225.0	8.3
1984-85	1,300.0	6.1
1985-86	1,189.1	-
1986-87	1,606.6	35.1
1987-88	1,856.1	15.5
1988-89	2,054.0	10.7
1989-90	2,386.0	16.2
1990-91	2,612.5	9.5
1991-92	4,892.0	87.3
1992-93	6,060.0	23.9
1993-94	6,970.3	15.0
1994-95	7,423.8	6.5
1995-96	9,150.3	23.3
1996-97	10,417.6(P)	13.8
1997-98	11,263.9(P)	8.1

* Figures for the years 1985-86 onwards were estimated on the basis of revised methodology and hence not comparable with those up to the year 1984-85.

(P) Provisional

Table 2.2

Summary of International Tourist Traffic to India during the Years 1981 to 1997

Year	*(Including nationals of Pakistan & Bangladesh)* Number	Per cent Change
1981	1279210	—
1982	1288162	0.7
1983	1304976	1.3
1984	1193752	-8.5
1985	1259384	5.5
1986	1451076	15.2
1987	1484290	2.3
1988	1590661	7.2
1989	1736093	9.1
1990	1707158	-1.7
1991	1677508	-1.7
1992	1867651	11.3
1993	1764830	-5.5
1994	1886433	6.9
1995	2123683	12.6
1996	2287860	7.7
1997	2374094	3.8

3

Regional Perspective—Two Cases

All the policy documents on tourism in India have emphasised the importance of preservation of cultural heritage and its enrichment through tourism. At the same time, quite often, serious concern is expressed about the 'adverse social impact of tourism'. Experiences around the world have confirmed that insensitive promotion of tourism in areas of fragile social and cultural ethos have often produced undesirable results. Striking a balance between the positive aspects of tourism in helping revival, regeneration and strengthening of culture and heritage and the possible negative impact flowing from demands placed by tourism promotion, is a perennial problem faced by the policy-planners.

Ladakh area in Jammu & Kashmir State of India is unique in its natural beauty. The old Buddhist monasteries with their distinctive designs and beautiful paintings, provide Ladakh with a rich cultural heritage. Ladakh has become an increasingly attractive tourist destination and the small communities tucked away in the foot hills of the Himalayan and the Karakoram ranges are suddenly becoming aware of the commercial potentials of their heritage. A study of the implications of 'heritage tourism' in Ladakh, therefore, is very pertinent in the context of the questions raised about social impact of tourism. The first part of this chapter examines these issues.

Similarly, while India as a whole plans and promotes international tourism within the constraints that we have already noticed, many of the far-flung areas of immense beauty and great tourism attractions run the risk of being left out unless tourism plans for such regions are dovetailed into the national and international requirements. Regional development of tourism has to be based on plans which are pragmatic, related to the requirement of domestic tourism and coordinated with the overall socio-economic plan for the region. Such a balanced and integrated development of tourism, for example, is the need of the North-Eastern region of India. The region which evokes so much of interest in tourists because of the variety of its attractions has yet to fully develop its tourism potentials.

Against this background of regional development perspectives, the scenario of tourism development of Assam, one of the seven States of the North-East, is briefly examined in the second part of the chapter.

HERITAGE PRESERVATION AND PLANNING FOR ECO SUSTAINABLE TOURISM IN LADAKH

"A people without history
Is not redeemed from time,
for history is a pattern
Of timeless moments"

—*T.S. Eliot : Four Quartets*

The experience of Ladakh is in fact an experience of such timeless moments. It seems as if time past and time future merges here in those timeless creations. It would be inappropriate, therefore, to try to confine such experience into the bounds of a rigorous definition. At the same time, any discussion on the heritage of Ladakh will remain incomplete unless it goes beyond the academic refinements into the hard realities of their sustainability in future. For the discussion to be so action-oriented, it is necessary to have a clear perception about the term 'heritage' itself.

Concept

The concept of 'heritage' is not a static one and has undergone changes over the years, particularly during the last two centuries. The Hague Convention, adopted by UNESCO in 1954, is perhaps the first international agreement on the subject. It defines "cultural property" irrespective of origin or ownership as covering several types of properties, for example, "movable or immovable property of great importance to the cultural heritage of every people, such as monuments or architecture, art and history, whether religious or secular; archaeological sites, groups of buildings, which, as a whole, are of historical or artistic interests"[1]. The UNESCO has provided a number of recommendations to Member States for the definition and management of cultural heritage. The World Heritage Convention (1972) and the Nairobi Recommendation (1976) "concerning the safeguarding and contemporary role of historical areas" are important landmarks. The Nairobi recommendation sees "heritage beyond single monuments or sites" and places emphasis on "social-economic context". It puts heritage in a global context which has to be "seen as a balanced whole, where the specific nature depends on the fusion of its parts and where human activities are one of its essential components"[2]. This recommendation underscores the important issue in heritage promotion and conservation, that it should be considered in its totality within the overall social-economic framework and not in isolation.

We can very briefly mention some of the salient features of heritage tourism which need to be kept in view while discussing its relevance to specific areas like Ladakh. First, of course, is the importance of the understanding that the heritage issue needs to be tackled, as stated above, in its comprehensive entirety, in the context of the socio-economic ethos of the area and not as conservation of heritage *per se*. The importance of such a perception finds endorsement in most of the discussions on the subject, e.g. :

> "Conceiving cultural heritage in the widest perspective shows its intimate connection with the general economic and land use planning of the society. This also means that policies for protection, conservation and rehabilitation of cultural resources should be understood as an essential part of the global policies and strategies for planning and management of the changing world".[3]

> "An overall development master plan incorporating both preservation and development concerns is required for the guidance of all.[4]"

> "For the conservation of a historic town to be most effective, it should be an integral part of a coherent policy of economic and social development and of urban and regional planning."[5]

Sustainable Ecotourism

In other words, the heritage issues need to be discussed in the overall context of sustainable development and not in isolation. The concept of 'sustainable development' naturally goes much beyond heritage only. The Brundtland Commission (the World Commission on Environment and Development) in its Statement in 1987, entitled 'Our Common Future', defined 'sustainable development' as "development that meets the needs of the present without compromising the ability of the future generation to meet their own needs". Inevitability of change and the need for development and a concern that change and development may adversely affect what nature and history have endowed this area with, overshadows most discussions on heritage tourism in Ladakh. Quite legitimate concerns have been expressed about the process of economic globalization "helping to destroy the existing fabric of local economy and community."[6] Sometimes, the concern goes to the extent of suggesting "counter development" measures. In Ladakh today, there is an imperative need for striking a balance between such extreme views and for regulating development and guiding change in a manner that sustainable development is possible.

Such a balanced view should start with an objective assessment of the possible impact of heritage tourism. Heritage, it is acknowledged, can be a means of socio-economic development of the area through tourism. Culture and heritage are prime attractions for foreign tourists visiting India. It can also be a means of promoting cultural understanding and of widening cultural horizons of the people who experience such cultural heritage through tourism. Experiences around the globe also have shown that tourism can stimulate the local economy by, among others, reviving and sustaining the traditional art and craft, which are integral part of the heritage of the area.

With the world fast becoming a 'global village', concern about tourism changing the values and attitudes of the younger generation of Ladakhis is understandable, but such concern sometimes overshadows the beneficial impact of tourism in creating awareness among the local people about their own culture. Such imperceptible beneficial impacts are widely accepted— "the concept of 'world heritage' is promoted by UNESCO while everywhere locals, often for the first time, look to their own particular patrimony, not least in economic hope."[7]

In this scenario, it is quite educative to look at the perception of the Ladakhis themselves, and also of those who are interested in preservation of Ladakh's heritage, about the major problems that tourism can create for them. The Public Hearing on Environment and Development organised by the People's Commission on Environment and Development in Leh on 23rd August, 1996 and the recommendations of the seminar on "Tourism Development" on 17th-18th September, 1995 at Leh highlighted the major problems that tourism creates for Ladakh and, for that matter, for other such heritage sites. The importance of the role of tourism in boosting self-confidence and pride of a people is often not realised, but this aspect has been forcefully brought out in the seminar by Sonam Wangchuk (in the Public Hearing in Leh)—"but there are two totally contradictory effects, one of consolidating and strengthening Ladakhi culture ... The direct interaction with people from developed and industrialised world, who had seen the darker side of modernization and were impressed by the sustainable lifestyles of Ladakh, acted as a most potent educational tool to revive the self-confidence and culture pride of Ladakhis."[8]

The foremost concern that comes out in all the discussions is the debasement of values and distortion of culture caused by the inroad of commercial tourism. This conflict can come in a number of ways. First, as it happened in the case of Ladakh, when an area opens up to tourists and many commercially lucrative avenues emerge, if the local population are unable to cater to all of them, pressure of population and unemployment elsewhere will lure outsiders to come and exploit those avenues. In one of the lead papers in the Public Hearing in Leh, Sonam Wangchuk, Director, Student's Educational and Cultural Movement[9] gives vent to the deep anguish of a Ladakhi in such a situation. "The pressure is not only from tourists but also from an influx of thousands of tourism-related workers who come from all parts of India. Due to the short and non-involved nature of their stay, none of them care about the fate of the place ... The magnitude of the problem nowadays often makes one feel ashamed to receive foreign friends in Leh."

The second danger of distortion of culture and heritage emerges from the necessity of catering to the needs of tourism as an industry, of promoting the heritage products to conform to the demands of the market. The impact is almost imperceptible but the problem is genuine and the dangers real, as shown by Boniface and Fowler, through a number of illustrations from real life experiences. They ask the fundamental questions "To cater successfully to tourists from other cultures, a producer must avoid offending his customers. His product must be 'market-led'. But how much will his product have to be fashioned in an alien image to suit his audience? And in satisfying one market, will another be repelled?"[10]

Analysing Impact of Tourism : Cultural Clash and Conflict

The most serious concern about the impact of tourism on the culture and heritage of Ladakh, flows from what Boniface and Fowler call 'culture clash'. They quote Ogilvy, who way back in 1983, in his book 'Ogilvy on Advertising' reporting how the Greeks prayed to the Almighty to spare them from the 'Scourge' of foreign tourism. Wood and House put the problem very clearly—"inevitably, constant contact with alien customs and cultures results in a weakening of native tradition and values."[11] The World Tourism Leaders' Meeting on Social Impacts of Tourism held in Manila on 22nd May, 1997 also echoed this concern. "The development of tourism will inevitably affect the culture of a host community; to what extent, will depend on a range of factors. Perhaps the most important is the cultural resilience of the host community and how it can meet the needs and expectations of the tourist without sacrificing its own traditions and values."[12]

Cultural and social change takes place through a number of factors, slowly over a period of time. Tourism is not necessarily the primary change agent, particularly in this age where technological and information revolution have reduced the world to a global village. But, protecting cultural heritage from over-enthusiastic and insensitive tourists, both domestic and foreign, is a problem which in case of Ladakh also needs to be handled carefully and urgently. The concept of a global village deceptively conceals very wide variations in culture. Tourism brings together people of such widely different cultural backgrounds and sensitivities. Quite often, ignorance of tourists' affects the sensitivity of local people; more often, insensitivity flowing from ignorance results in modes of behaviour which may even affect preservation of the products. The "away from home syndrome" of short-term tourists may be another contributing factor to the emergence of socio-cultural conflict with the spread of tourism in an area like Ladakh otherwise insulated from invasion of modernism.

It is obvious from the references in the discussion papers and also from the discussion notes of both the Public Hearing in Ladakh and the seminar referred to earlier, that Ladakh today is faced with a similar situation. And in similar situations elsewhere in the world, the emerging solution was to try to educate the tourists, to guide them sensitively and to interpret the nuances in culture through professionals. Educating the tourists and bringing about attitudinal change, however, is not an easy job. It requires use of technological innovations, sustained efforts and trained manpower. These are the areas in which tourism in Ladakh needs to concentrate on in future.

Such cultural conflict has another dimension which is also relevant to Ladakh. Most of the heritage sites are in rural pastoral settings sustained by the community ethos of an agricultural community with deep cultural moorings in the heritage around them. Such heritage grew with their tender care and craftmanship. Change and development have affected these rural attachments and social commitments to the heritage. The Public Hearing in Ladakh and in particular the lead paper of Helena Norberg-Hodge[13] and Janet Rizvi[14] point out that development has changed the agricultural system and social structures in Ladakh. With the shift in economic power to the urban areas, rural-based heritage has lost the nucleus of support system and starved of such support heritage management has of necessity to make compromises on commercial consideration. Development of heritage tourism itself for such products, located in rural areas presents some inherent problems. Boniface and Fowler[15] put the problem succinctly—"how is it best to present a rural attraction to an audience largely soaked in urban life ways? ... how can the essential rural nature of a countryside be preserved when tourist needs require the trappings of suburbia or town centre—large parks for cars, ... cafes and convenience, good access roads ... ?"

Any tourism development plan has to be concerned about providing such basic facilities. In a situation like that of Ladakh, with perennial shortage of civic amenities, tourism development may have immediately two-fold effect. First, it will put further pressure on the already stressed infrastructure. "As over-crowding occurs, the host community may find itself under greater pressure from visitors, a pressure which may change the rhythms of a community's lifestyle."[16] It causes irritation to the local public and this sense of irritation runs through prominently in all the discussions on Leh referred to earlier. Secondly, such irritation aggravates when priority is given to the needs of the tourists, giving rise to what Jenkins calls 'irridex effect'. In such a situation, often solution is sought in trying to determine, what is generally called the 'carrying capacity' of the product and attempting to regulate the number of tourists. Such an attempt in fact is a recognition of the existence of a conflict between the temptation that tourism offers for maximum commercial exploitation and the need for preserving such heritage for future generation. Basically, it is a question of balancing present economic gains with long term interest of future sustainability. It is not surprising that the seminar on "Tourism and Environment" held in Leh (17th-18th September, 1995) thus recommended—

"There is an urgent need to fix a ceiling for tourist traffic to the area. Steps should be taken to fix an upper ceiling of 25-30 thousand tourists per year so that the traffic is related with the existing carrying capacity, human and material resources and availability of supplies."[17]

It is also interesting to note that the UNESCO Workshop on Sustainable Tourism Development in World Heritage Sites —"Planning for Hue" has the following basic overriding recommendation which amplifies the general conflict between tourism development and sustainable needs—

"Over-arching all of the specific recommendations... is the general observation that the overwhelming majority of the participants felt that the projected target of 10,00,000 tourists per year by the year 2000 is far too high to be realistic, manageable or sustainable. Such a number may well exceed the carrying capacity of the monuments and also the capacity of the infrastructure."[18] The resolution goes on to explain the possible effects on infrastructure and environment and emphasizes the need for pursuing quality of tourists rather than quantity.

Heritage Preservation and Sustainable Tourism Promotion

Leaving aside the cultural dimensions of heritage tourism, one has to look at the important question of preservation of the heritage products. The preservation of heritage again can have many dimensions, e.g. physical, technical, artistic and socio-economic. The physical aspects of conservation would primarily relate to, —

(a) structural engineering;
(b) construction and design suited to local environment; and
(c) use of materials which suit the local climatic conditions and blend aesthetically with the surroundings.

Similarly, preservation of the artistic and technical ingredients may relate to firstly, preservation of the art work, paintings, carvings, etc., by using modern technology and preventing further deterioration; and, secondly, where restoration is needed, use of such technology which maintains the original authenticity and also ensures that no damage is caused. The importance of authenticity in preservation of heritage cannot be over-emphasized. "Tourism is" say Louis Turner and John Ash "everywhere the enemy of authenticity and cultural identity."[19] 'Planning for Hue', therefore, amplifies authenticity to mean: authenticity in form and design; authenticity in materials and technology; authenticity in function and use; authenticity in context, setting and 'spirit'.

UNESCO has carried out specific studies in different heritage sites on the problems of their conservation. In one such workshop relating to Sustainable Tourism Development in World Heritage Sites—Planning for Hue in Vietnam, the following basic recommendations emerged[20]:

- Need to assure cultural authenticity in all preservation, conservation and restoration work.
- Need for overall development of a master plan for the area, incorporating both preservation and development concerns.
- To ascertain the carrying capacity of each product and regulate the number of visitors where required.
- To take up meaningful human resource development programmes, including training of guides and tour operators and also involving measures for educating the tourists on the cultural sensitivities.
- Steps to involve the local community so that they take pride in what they have and can take pleasure in maintaining them, and also share the benefits of tourism development.
- Need for innovative private-public partnership so that resources could be mobilised to the maximum extent possible, for sustainable development.

The Manila Declaration following the World Tourism Leaders' Meeting on the Social Impacts of Tourism also echoes these issues as the basis for future action. *(Appendix V)*

The actions required for preservation of heritage and its promotion in Ladakh, can be summed up as follows— first, of course, is the necessity of immediate attention to preservation of many of the heritage products like the monasteries which are in a very precarious state of conservation. There is some urgency in this regard. Along with the steps for preservation of the structure of some of these heritage monuments, the exquisite wall paintings and the decorations as well as the carvings in many of the monasteries also need to be carefully renovated and preserved. This important work of conservation of the heritage products may involve the following stages :

- Documentation of the present condition of the heritage products.
- Assessment of the work required to be taken up, indicating the type of structural work, artistic work and technical preservation work.
- Prioritisation of the work to be taken up.
- Selection of technically competent persons and institutions to take up the work.
- Involving the local people in the entire exercise of identification of the problems and finding solutions to them.

This is a job which needs to be taken up urgently. However, as has already been mentioned, this job cannot be taken up in isolation. As a long-term strategy, this comprehensive plan for promotion and preservation of the heritage of Ladakh must be dovetailed into an overall socio-economic development plan for the area. In such a plan, tourism may be used as an agent for creating local-based sources for generation of income and employment. Such plans will remain only on paper unless resources are identified and made available. If we have to depend only on government resources for taking up such activities, the plans may never effectively take off. One has, therefore, to look beyond government funding and look for involvement of private sector and for public-private collaboration. Ladakh today in this regard faces a special problem. All such special problems need special attention and solutions. One such solution could be to create a 'development fund' for preservation and promotion of heritage in Ladakh. Government support can provide the nucleus for such a fund but it can be sustained only through involvement of committed institutions and agencies who can look beyond the present. The operation of the fund also would be an important organisational input which should be taken care of from the beginning. To make this idea a reality, we have to identify some agency who would act as a catalyst for getting other committed agencies involved.

For any conspicuous activity to really take place and be effective, one must have in place a proper organisation. Such an organisation must involve those whose feelings and association are vital for the survival of such heritage. We will have to involve the people around the heritage products, the monks in the monasteries and the others who have their sustenance and livelihood around those monasteries. Apart from usual publicity programmes taken up through government agencies, the town of Leh could be made the focal point for orientation of tourists before they come into personal contact with the heritage products. Leh is the first contact point for most people coming to Ladakh and they do look for information and ideas. There has been some mention about creating a museum in Leh which will give a glimpse of art, craft, tradition and the lifestyle of people in Ladakh through innovative technological inputs. Such a concept of museum, however, has to go beyond the normal concept of just storing some artifact without imagination. I would like to quote what Boniface and Fowler mention about what a museum should be. "Alessandro Mendini, has said : 'A museum should be an invention, an ideal place abounding in surprises, not a necrophiliac depository of cultural power'. Artist Frank Stell has said : 'The building works in a parallel way with my wavy, Moby Dick series. You move through this New Wave Museum as though making a voyage'. And Philippe Starch has said 'This museum is like a ghost train—at every stage you find a surprise. Intuition prepares you for enlightenment, not audio-visual lectures. There's less to read, more to feel'."

Conclusion

Anything of the nature outlined above to take place would need people who are motivated, who are professionally trained and who have acquired the technical expertise. So, human resource development would be a key element of the master plan for development of heritage tourism in Ladakh. Such development will be slightly different from the usual training programmes and should be developed to suit the local requirements. It should include training of professionals to guide people about the heritage of Ladakh, training of people to be involved in the preservation and renovation work where needed, and training of people who while being involved in their normal agricultural activities would also be enthused about maintenance of ecology. This could be the beginning of a process of heritage preservation and planning for eco-sustainable tourism in Ladakh which is truly sustainable and in which the people can take pride and from which the people can benefit. We have to make this beginning.

TOURISM AS AN AGENT OF CHANGE AND DEVELOPMENT IN THE STATE OF ASSAM : SOME THOUGHTS

Assam is one of the seven States in North-East of India. The seven States—Arunachal Pradesh, Assam, Manipur, Meghalaya, Mizoram, Nagaland and Tripura, are popularly called the 'Seven Sisters'. Assam, which has common borders with all the other States, is also the most thickly populated accounting for more than 70 per cent population of the North-East. The economic scenario of Assam over the last 50 years has a very complex and paradoxical story. Richly endowed with natural resources — oil reserves, coal, rich forests, fertile agricultural land, a large number of tea gardens — yet it is a picture of poverty amidst plenty. Assam's per capita income in constant prices which was higher than the national average in 1951 has been continuously falling behind ever since, and is now much below the national average. During the '90s when the national economy was growing between 4-6 per cent per annum, Assam's growth rate was only 2.9 per cent. Manufacturing growth between 1991- 92 and 1995- 96 was negative {-0.1per cent} and agriculture a meagre 1.2 per cent.[21] Such a state of affairs can only imply that the income generating activities in the State have been negligible. At the same time, the actual outgo of income from the region, and from Assam in particular, is very huge. Food products import alone is estimated to be around Rs. 1500 crores every year for Assam.[22] All this paints a very grim scenario for Assam. Such economic stagnation has contributed to the overall situation of despondency, alienation and unrest. In an effort to rectify the situation before it gets completely out of hand, a number of steps have been taken and many reports submitted about action needed. The High Level Commission constituted by the Government of India in its report to the Prime Minister has touched upon a large number of issues for the development of the region. However, tourism as such does not find the focus of attention that it should have as a strategy of income and employment generation. The Committee's recommendation that a Tourism Development Corporation should be set up is rather old fashioned and it touches only the fringe of the issues and offers only pedestrian solutions. Such a recommendation for an institutional set-up is surprising because at the national level, the move now is for disinvesting in the Government Corporations. The North East Council (NEC) itself has two corporations which reportedly are just pushing along without any impact. Assam had 48 corporations in 1994-95 and of these only three were running in profit. The total accumulated loss to the corporations was Rs. 1500 crores.[23] In such a scenario adding one more corporation is hardly likely to provide the income and employment generation scope.

The employment potential of tourism alone makes it necessary to look at tourism as a possible means of regeneration of economic activities in Assam. Any development plan for Assam in the backgound of the State's present socio-economic situation should—

(a) make an assessment of the ground realities, assess the constraints and make efforts to overcome them;

(b) build on the comparative advantage of the region rather than routinely try to emulate the successful development models of other areas; and

(c) focus on the urgent need to create income and employment as, at present, there has been hardly any income generating investment in the State except minimal investment made out of the Plan Budget. Massive private investment can give a kick-start to the economy. But present economic trends and socio-political developments indicate that such a spurt in economic activities in the private sector is unlikely to materialise quickly. At the same time, because internal economic activities have been limited, substantial portion of income is being spent on paying for imports from other regions. The multiplier effect, speaking crudely, is negative. It is essential, therefore, to look at the alternative ways of creating income and employment.

Tourism fits into this scenario very well. It is in this sector that Assam has comparative advantage over many other regions. By way of illustration, one can mention a few advantages that Assam enjoys :

(i) Natural beauty of immense variety.

(ii) A colourful mosaic of cultures of numerous tribes and ethnic identities, making it a unique place for anthropological adventures.

(iii) Varied and interesting wild-life and beautiful national parks, which have rare animal specimens like the one-horned rhinoceros, etc.

(iv) The hills and vales, the mighty river Brahmaputra with innumerable tributaries, and nature's abundant variety provide ample scope for adventure tourism.

(v) Assam also has a very rich cultural-religious heritage. Numerous mythological folk lores link Assam to the great epic, *Mahabharata.* Deeply venerated places like the Kamakhya Temple, the seat of Tantric learnings take Assam's cultural history even beyond those periods.

(vi) Arts and craft are a way of life with a large mumber of people in Assam. Handicrafts and handlooms of distinctive beauty, like the 'golden thread'—'muga' give Assam a unique advantage in promoting ethnic craft related tourism.

However, at present, the number of tourists coming to Assam is negligible. The available figures show that even the number of domestic tourists have come down from 17,649 in 1994 to 14,443 in 1996 whereas the number of foreign tourists has not even crossed the figure of 1,000. It is quite possible that the method of compilation of statistics has not correctly reflected the number of actual arrivals. Even if the methodology was corrected, the actual number is not likely to be substantially more than what is reported so far. In any case, the true potentials of the State are much higher.

Any action plan for the development of tourism in the region must start with an objective self-assessment. There are problems in plenty, and the planning process must recognise the problems and take them into consideration. Often, however, there is a tendency to overlook the problems and a tendency to assume that the beauty of the place and its attractions would automatically bring in tourists. The starting point of any action plan, therefore, should be a close look at the strengths and weaknesses as the tourists would see them.

More and more tourists all over the world today travel for leisure and relaxation. It is observed that what a tourist looks for most is an ambience where he can relax and enjoy his holiday free from tension and worries. Unfortunately, because of various reports emanating from the area about ethnic clashes, occasional violence, etc., the outside world has at present, a picture of Assam as an unsettled place which is to be avoided. Marketing and promotional measures can only go part of the way in creating an image. In the final analysis, there is no substitute for a visitor's happy experience. This is an area where Assam needs to put maximum attention for the correction of its image.

Some of the other commonly observed constraints to development of tourism in Assam are—

(a) Poor communication linkages with Assam and the region and also within it.

(b) Condition of tourism infrastructure is generally poor. The roads are slow and inadequate, wayside amenities almost non-existent, or where they exist, they lack in quality, cleanliness and hygiene, and most places do not have decent, affordable lodgings of reasonable standard. The need for trained manpower is acutely felt in all areas.

(c) There are not sufficient resources for substantial government investment required to improve infrastructure. It is necessary, therefore, to make investment selectively in key areas and also to look for greater private collaboration in tourism development.

It is generally said in the tourism sector that "tourism is what everyone talks about but no one cares". Any action plan for the development of tourism must, therefore, start from the grass roots and must be based on a commonsense approach. In such an action plan, some of the ideas that could be kept uppermost are :

(i) Tourism has to be given priority in the thinking process of the government. The importance of tourism as an input in the development process must be adequately appreciated and awareness about it should be created among policy-makers, bureaucrats and the people in general. Even in resource allocation, at present tourism is being accorded very low priority.

(ii) As resources are limited, an attempt should be made to ensure the most efficient use of the existing resources. For this purpose, areas of primary attraction like the Kaziranga National Park and other wildlife sanctuaries, religious places like Kamakhya, water and adventure sports in Brahmaputra, etc., should be identified and fully developed instead of spreading the resources thinly on many small projects. In tune with the national policy, the State Government should identify a few circuits and take up development in a planned manner around those circuits.

(iii) Initially it would, in fact, be most cost-effective to concentrate on plans for infrastructure development for domestic tourists. Once the tourist flow starts, it will generate income and employment, and the process of economic activity will start. As more people visit, positive publicity may start, setting in motion a self-generating process of development. That may attract more private initiative and generate resources for infrastructure development to attract more foreign tourists. Domestic tourism should be the foundation on which tourism development plans of the State should be built. It will be futile to create heavy infrastructure facilities in expectation of flow of foreign tourists. Creation of infrastructure in still underdeveloped areas like Assam can be economically and commercial viable only when they are built on local demand. In a sense, in such a richly endowed area like Assam promotion of tourism can be 'supply-led'.

(iv) As the area suffers from communication difficulties, it would be a good strategy to develop a portfolio of attractions through regional cooperation among the States of the region so that each one can gain from the strength of others in the region.

(v) Government should take the lead in facilitating greater private collaboration. This can be done by a variety of measures, designed to provide incentives and aimed to remove the obstacles to the growth of private enterprise.

(vi) As communication to Assam and inside the region is a major bottleneck, steps to make access to the State and the region easier should be at the top of the agenda of the State and National

Governments. For too long the region has suffered from a feeling of neglect, primarily because of the distance from the centre of power. Better communication will go a long way in removing this feeling of alienation. In concrete terms, the Report of the Task Force on the North-East has this to say :[24]

> "Poor accessibility is yet another impediment. The airports are mostly small with minimum equipments and are incapable of handling large aircrafts. The present level of traffic flow to these airports also do not justify the operation of large aircrafts. Thus, most of the domestic airlines operating in India are not capable of introducing air services to these airports as they do not have small aircraft of requisite capacity. The operation of such aircraft are also generally not economically viable due to high cost of fuel and other inputs. The region is also not easily accessible by rail except Assam. Roads and road-transport systems are weak and not very much tourism friendly."
>
> "Guwahati may be made a regional hub for 'Alliance Airlines' with a group of at least 5 small aircraft so that they can operate regular and chartered flights to various airports in the region. The feasibility of establishing a separate subsidiary company with the participartion of all the State Governments in the region for such air services can also be considered by the Deparment of Civil Aviation."

(vii) Immediate steps could be taken to develop a number of tourist spots around places like Guwahati, so that people have opportunity to spend holidays and weekends at leisure. Such spots can be developed all along the National Highway. Such local movements may be the first fillip to the development of tourist facilities and improvement of the tourist products.

(viii) Kaziranga National Park is a major attraction of the State and all attention has been concentrated here. But one attraction cannot bring tourists all the way, ignoring all problems of communication. The attractions have to be diversified and developed. Tourists feel lost after a visit to Kaziranga Game Sanctuary, having nothing else to do. Package tours to include a visit to the exotic tea-gardens, golfing, a cruise down Brahmaputra, touching other game sanctuaries or unique places of pilgrimage like Hajo where a mosque and a temple exist side-by-side, may liven up the tourism prospects.

There are many other things one can do. If one dares to dream, other things fall in place. We need vision and determination to translate such vision into action.

For development of tourism in Assam and for making it a catalyst for economic regeneration, Assam needs to draw up a comprehensive plan of action and time-bound implementation. Initially, the government will have to play the pioneering role of promoting, regulating and also facilitating greater private enterprise. The government will also have to take the lead to create awareness about the potentials of tourism. Only from such awareness can a tourist-friendly culture grow.

From Assam's experience in tourism development, a few conclusions can be drawn which can be true of most of other States as well :

(i) Even though the Five Year Plans have accepted a selective development approach as a strategy, and at the national level, special areas and circuits were identified, such selective and concentrated efforts are not in evidence in the State level planning. Scarce resources are distributed thinly over too many schemes to satisfy the local demands. As has been mentioned elsewhere the Five Year Plans also make a distinction between the Central Government support for infrastructure development and those of the State Government. It was a well defined strategy that Central assistance would be utilised in the development of destinations which have national importance and which attract both domestic and foreign tourists. State budgetary resources were to be utilised more for the development of local products. No such conscious planning is seen. Admittedly, no clear dichotomy in the development of destinations is possible. But, even a semblance of an effort towards such a rational approach is missing in the planning strategy.

(ii) The budgetary support for the development of infrastructure in tourism has been negligible in most cases. As a percentage of the total budget, allocation to tourism has been much lower in the States than it is in the Centre. As a result, in most cases, the Central assistance which is to be used only as supplementary resources, has become the main source of financing tourism development.

(iii) In Assam, as in most of the cases, the development of tourism is seen as a responsibility of the Department of Tourism and, therefore, the tourism development plans are not integrated at district levels. Tourism, in fact, is not seen in the field as a common endeavour.

(iv) There is no mechanism for public participation in tourism development. Tourism development continues as implementation of isolated schemes of the Department of Tourism and not as a spontaneous thrust area within an integrated economic development policy.

(v) Nor is there any evidence of substantial private participation. The initiative seems to be lacking from both the sides. And, though tourism is eulogized as a private sector driven industry, in reality, it is predominantly dependent on the Government as the prime mover.

References

1. Dr Jukka, Jokilehto (1995), Specialist Seminar on the Management Guidelines of World Cultural Heritage Sites. In the proceedings of *3rd International Symposium of World Heritage Cities*, Bergen, June 28-30, p. 93.
2. *Ibid*, p. 94.
3. *Ibid*, p. 94.
4. UNESCO, (1995), "Planning for Hue". In the proceedings of the *Workshop on Sustainable Tourism Development in World Heritage Sites* - Hue, Vietnam, 3-6 May, p. 2.
5. Krishna Menon, A.G., *Cultural Identity and Urban Development* - INTACH, 1989, p. 6.
6. Public Hearing on Environment and Development, Leh, August 23, (1996), The People's Commission on Environment and Development, India, particularly the lead paper *"Development and Change in Ladakh"* Helena Norberg - Hodge, pp. 4-6.
7. Princilla Boniface and Peter J. Fowler, (1993), *Heritage and Tourism*, p. 154, Routledge.

8. Public Hearing on Environment and Development (1996), Leh, August 23, *op. cit*, p. 22.
9. Public Hearing on Environment and Development (1996), Leh, August, 23, *op. cit.* p. 21.
10. Boniface and Fowler, *op. cit.* p. 4.
11. Wood, K and House, S (1991), *The Good Tourist*, London, Mandarin, p. 28.
12. Jenkins, C.L. Prof. (1997), Social Impacts of Tourism - Background paper in *World Tourism Leaders' Meeting on Social Impacts of Tourism, Manila*, 27th May, in Final Report, WTO. p. 16.
13. Helena Norberg - Hodge, *op. cit.* pp. 4-6.
14. Rizvi, Janet (1996), "*Change and Development in Ladakh : An Overview*" in Public Hearing on Environment and Development, *op. cit.* pp. 7-9.
15. Boniface and Fowler, *op. cit.* pp. 78-79.
16. Jenkins, C.L., op. cit. p. 17.
17. Recommendations (No. 5) of the Seminar on *Tourism and Development*, September 17-18, 1995, Leh.
18. UNESCO, *op. cit.* p. 7.
19. Turner, Louis and Ash John, (1975) "*The Golden Hordes : International Tourism and the Pleasure Periphery*", London, Constable, p. 197 (quoted by Boniface).
20. UNESCO, *op. cit.* pp. 1-6.
21. Gulshan Sachdeva : "Assam economy : Past, present & future" in Peace Initiative Vol. IV No.I-II January-April, 1998, p. 39.
22. *Ibid.*, p. 41.
23. Sachdeva : *op cit.* p. 43.
24. Report of the Task Force on Development of Tourism in the North Eastern India. Ministry of Tourism.

4

Public-Private Partnership

The theme adopted by the World Tourism Organization for celebration of the World Tourism Day, 1998 was 'Public-private partnership'. This is a significant development, and in a sense a symbolic one. This concept of partnership implies a shift away from strong Central Government intervention to a more constructive participatory approach. Since the early 1980s the world has witnessed a political and economic shift towards market-driven economies and ideas of economic liberalisation and privatisation have gained momentum. This changing climate has affected tourism administration across the globe as well. The nature and extent of government involvement in tourism varies widely from country to country but even within such variations there are unmistakable signs of realisation everywhere that the responsibilities in management of tourism should be rationally shared between the private and the public sectors. This increasing role and meaningful voice of the private sector in the management of tourism is not dictated only by the constraints of the public sector budgets. New mechanisms and new structures are being tried to forge links between the private sector and government to tackle widely diverse problems of tourism management.

The Concept of 'Partnership'

The idea of 'partnership' goes much beyond the generally used expression of 'private participation'. Such partnership implies systems of formalised cooperation between the public (government) and private sectors where the partners share responsibilities, resources, risks and rewards. The rationale for such partnership is implicit in the very trends of the present-day tourism developments. Over the years, demand for tourism products and services has grown significantly and such demands, as we have seen, are likely to increase manifold within a very short span of time in the future.

Developments in information technology will make access to information easier. And because the competition will be sharp, countries will provide prospective tourists with wider options. Those countries which can respond quickly to changing consumer demands will naturally have an edge over others. By the very nature of functioning, the government systems are more rigid and less responsive to emerging situations than the functioning of private organisations. Partnership strengthens the country's efforts in the international arena.

At the same time, sources of government funding, particularly for tourism related areas, are slowly declining all over the world. In countries like India, the pressures on limited resources is even more acute because along with declining sources of revenue, there are increasing demands for quickly satisfying the basic needs of the people for health, education, drinking water, etc. One major objective of partnership is to make more resources available for tourism without depending too heavily on larger budgetary support.

The objectives of such partnership, therefore, can vary from country to country. But some of the areas where such partnership could be meaningful are, —

(a) financing of new infrastructure development projects;

(b) devising more attractive means of sustainable development;

(c) evolving a modern, focussed, comprehensive and intensive marketing collaboration;

(d) improving quality in services through human resource development;

(e) participating in the preservation of the very fragile heritage; and

(f) development and beautification of various tourism products.

The list can go on. The requirement of each country will decide the extent and the depth of such partnership and general prescriptions can always run the risk of being irrelevant. There is no doubt that when the partners realise the commonality of objectives and put the relationship into a systematic format, the pooling of expertise, experience and resources will benefit both the partners. For a successful programme of such partnership, continuous and pragmatic understanding is essential. Such continuous understanding can be achieved if the relationship is systemic and not ad hoc. Such systemic relationship will be facilitated by, —

(i) clear planning of roles and integration of respective roles;

(ii) clarity of the role of each partner;

(iii) identification of the benefits to each of the partners;

(iv) ensuring that there is no duplication of programmes and activities;

(v) laying down working parameters for long term commitment from either side; and

(vi) periodic evaluation of the efficacy of each other's role.

However, there are certain activities which by their very nature have to be performed by the government and cannot be delegated to any other agency. Tourism is a multi-sectoral activity and depends to a large extent on the healthy inter-relationship between the different components of the sectors. Only government measures can bring about the required coordination between such diverse but inter-related economic activities. Moreover, a country's tourism promotion is also influenced by the inter-dependence of the global economy and issues relating to such inter-dependence can be handled only by the government. The government policy on exchange-control, international relations, etc., has deep bearing on travel and tourism. At the same time, government support and encouragement to the private sector can be of vital importance for growth of tourism.

In brief, the government has the overall responsibility of laying down policies and ensuring proper planning to achieve those policy objectives. Policies normally indicate the broad 'directions of action'. The tourism policy should, among other things, indicate how tourism planning can be integrated with the overall development planning goals of the country.

Tourism being a multi-dimensional, multi-sectoral activity, the issues to be integrated and problems to be tackled are also complex. Therefore, the structure of solutions to the issues also vary from place to place. Such variety of objectives and approach inherent in the system, makes it more necessary to have a cohesive planning. Such planning should integrate marketing strategy, development of physical infrastructure, human resource development, international relationship, inter-sectoral linkages in national economic planning, facilitation for tourist's travels, security and safety — just to mention a few areas. Such integrated planning is needed to ensure that scarce resources are used to the optimal level. Only the government can provide comprehensive planning of this type which takes into account the total impact of tourism.

Within such a comprehensive planning, some specific areas need particular mention. The foremost responsibility of the government is in facilitating access of the tourists to the country. For a tourist, the first contact with the country is through the embassies for visa, and the customs and immigration on arrival. Therefore, the government policy in these areas and the effectiveness of the policies in creating a tourism-friendly atmosphere greatly influence the decisions of the intending travellers.

Within the country again, the ease of travel and availability of good infrastructure are crucial factors for promoting tourism. Creating congenial atmosphere and physical facilities that make travel pleasant and smooth, depend on many factors which are not always entirely within the control of the government. In India, traditionally the government had a pre dominant role in providing basic infrastructure like roads, power, telecommunications, railways, etc. The recent economic liberalisation policies have opened up these and many more areas for private participation. Foreign investments have been allowed in many sectors which were earlier exclusively reserved for the public sector only. Foreign equity participation up to 100 per cent in tourism infrastructure is now possible. As a result of such developments, while the primary role of promotion remains with the govenment, there is a qualitative change in this role. The new concept of partnership enjoins on the government the responsibility of creating an atmosphere which encourages a dynamic role of the private sector. Where private initiatives are lacking or are yet to develop, the government have to come forward to fill in the gap. In pursuance of this basic policy, the Government of India have initiated a number of incentives to the private sector in tourism industry.

With the liberalisation of economic policies, the Government of India have by and large, moved away from controls and regulations, of issues which are best decided by the market forces. There are, however, wide ranging issues in the tourism sector affecting consumer interests which require regulation and careful management. Out of such concern emerges the regulatory role of the government in protecting the environment, the cultural heritage and the consumers' interests.

India's growing population has already put a lot of pressure on its ecosystem. Tourist arrivals, both foreign and domestic, in large numbers, will undoubtedly increase this pressure, particularly in the frequently visited places of tourist interest. Therefore, the idea of sustainable development to be meaningful needs all the skills of government management and authority to enforce the norms. For protection of consumer interests, government have to enforce regulations on building and fire safety norms for hotels and other establishments, standards of health hygiene, tour safety and sanitation in places of tourist attractions, safety in transport operations, security of tourists, etc. In the next millennium, with the phenomenal growth of tourism around the world, the pressure on the air services and airspace will also increase tremendously. It is expected that the coming years will also witness remarkable advancement in aviation technology and safety standards to match the growing demands. Because of such pressure on the skies, the need for strict government regulations on aviation safety becomes all the more important.

Similarly, while the private sector is the most important motivator for bringing tourists to the country, the promotion of a national image has traditionally and primarily been the task of the government. Even when more and more national barriers are coming down, and various regional economic groupings are emerging, consumers' choice of destinations will be dependent on the national image that is created. Devising appropriate marketing strategies to promote a national image will remain the responsibility of the government.

However, tourism is an international activity that brings people from different countries together. India's tourism policy has always emphasised the role of tourism in promoting international understanding. Economically, as noted, it is emerging as the largest export industry in the world. It is only natural that the government have a key role to play in protecting the national interest and projecting national viewpoint in international settings. International trade agreements are extending to wider areas of economic activities. Hard bargaining and consummate diplomatic manoeuvres are necessary to protect a country's genuine interests in international fora. Such agreements have bearing on tourism-related issues as well. Sometimes, with the emergence of regional groupings while national barriers come down within the regions, the region itself may become a fortress in relation to the nations outside. In such a situation, the national government will have to play the role of protecting the country's interests, including the private sector against artificial barriers. In protecting and promoting the Indian private sector in the international arena, the government plays its role in many ways, though not always visible and not always easily defineable.

Just as the government's role in the partnership cannot be strictly defined, the role of the private sector in tourism development also cannot be placed in any straightjacket. The role that is envisaged for the government as above, itself points to the areas where the private sector has to play a dominant role in the collaboration.

The role the private sector plays, as mentioned, would be wide-spread and dictated by pragmatic market considerations. However, some of the salient areas for their role could be identified as follows —

(i) Quality of service being the key and the beneficiary of human resource development being the private sector, it should play a wider role in human resource development, Private sector could sponsor institutes or could take up training of trainer's schemes, etc.

(ii) While the government would basically try to promote the interests of the country, much more result-oriented promotion could be achieved if the private sector, which individually and separately is promoting its products, could coordinate its activities with the government. Such coordination will be more cost-effective and more result-oriented.

(iii) As India is now opening up more and more areas for private sector participation, wherever possible, the private sector should take a lead in filling up the infrastructure gaps in accommodation, transport, etc.

(iv) In all future activities, sustainable development or eco-tourism would be a key element. The private sector should provide the lead and examples in green practices.

(v) Similarly, creating awareness about the role of tourism and involving the local community in the promotion of tourism and in sharing the benefit of tourism are essential for the future. The private sector should take it as a motto to involve the people in all their activities.

(vi) The quality standard being of great importance, the private sector should take greater initiative in setting standards for themselves and for enforcing such norms on the members of their organizations.

(vii) Since there are too many players in the private sector, it always helps interactions if there could be one platform or an apex organisation of the private sector in tourism.

(viii) The industry should take the lead in identifying and diversifying new circuits of arrivals. For example, there is a need for looking at Japan and the Asia-Pacific region and to build contact and coordination with the government for promotion of such areas.

(ix) Most important, the private sector can take the lead to give a new direction to the mind-sets and to talk of tourism as a whole and move away from the dichotomy of 'government' and the 'private sector', to think about a public-private collaboration.

Every small step matters and every small achievement would ultimately build up the future. It is time for us to make a beginning off the beaten track, however small the beginning may be.

The Role of the Private Sector in the Indian Context

Till the Seventh Plan, the Five Year Plan documents had not touched on a specific role of the private sector in tourism or on the primary responsibility of the government in creating a congenial atmosphere where the private sector can play a dynamic role envisaged for them. The draft policy makes a refreshing reference to the role of the government in facilitating the growth of a dynamic private sector—refreshing, because this role being beyond the realm of the Ministry of Tourism implies some sort of national consensus to achieve this objective. The first economic policy statement of the Prime Minister, Mr Atal Behari Vajpayee in his address to the Confederaation of Indian Industries (CII) Annual Conference, where he talks of 'participative collaboration', is also a significant development from this point of view.[1]

One of the major objectives identified for the tourism sector in the Seventh Plan was :

> "Re-defining of the role of the public and private sectors to ensure that the private sector investment is encouraged in developing tourism and the public sector investment is focussed mainly on the development of support infrastructure."[2]

The Eighth Plan also recorded :

> "The future growth of tourism should, therefore, be achieved mainly through private initiative. The State can contribute to tourism by planning broad strategies of development, provision of fiscal and monetary incentives to catalyse private sector investments and by devising effective regulatory and supervisory mechanisms to protect the interests of the industry, the consumer and the environment."[3]

The Draft of the National Tourism Policy circulated in 1997 *(Appendix-III)* by the Government of India also identifies the role of the government and that of the private sector as follows:

Role of the Government

(i) To provide public infrastructural facilities including local planning and zoning arrangements.

(ii) To plan tourism development as a part of the overall area development strategy.

(iii) Creation of a nucleus infrastructure in the initial stages of development to demonstrate the potentials of the area.

(iv) Provide support facilities and facilitation services to private enterprises along with appropriate incentives and land policies.

(v) To introduce regulatory measures to ensure social, cultural and environmental sustainability.

(vi) To ensure that the type and scale of tourism development is compatible with the environment and socio-cultural milieu of the area.

(vii) To ensure that the local community is fully involved and the benefits of tourism also accrue to them.

(viii) To facilitate availability of trained manpower particularly from amongst the local population jointly with the industry.

(ix) To undertake research, prepare master plans, and facilitate formulation of marketing strategies.

(x) To organise overseas promotion and marketing jointly with the industry.

(xi) To facilitate the growth of a dynamic tourism sector.

Role of the Private Sector

(i) To build and manage the required tourist facilities in all places of tourist interest.

(ii) To assume collective responsibility for laying down industry standards, ethics and fair practices.

(iii) To ensure preservation and protection of tourist attractions and take lead in green practices.

(iv) To involve the local community in tourism projects and ensure that the benefits of tourism accrue to them in right measure.

(v) To undertake industry training and manpower development to achieve excellence in quality of services.

(vi) To participate in the preparation of investment guidelines and marketing strategies and assist in database creation and research.

(vii) To ensure the safety and security of tourists.

(viii) To endeavour to promote tourism on a sustained and long-term perspective.[4]

It is clear from these statements that there is at least in recent times a clear recognition of the role of the private sector in the development of tourism. It is significant that these statements speak of respective roles and not so much about the areas where the roles could converge. Such a dichotomy in perception is perhaps inherent in the overall philosophy of economic planning in India, where a role for the private sector has emerged only during the recent years.

This issue of public and private partnership has to be seen in the overall context of the general economic policies of the country. The process of the emergence of the private sector in India can be broken up into four clear phases as delineated below:

(1) ***Period of public monopoly or of the 'commanding heights' of the public sector:*** This period, starting from the beginning of planned economic development in the 1950s, roughly continued till 1970. This was a period in which the activities in the tourism sector, as in almost every other sector of the economy were marked by preponderance of ownership and management of tourism by the State.

This development was marked by two prominent factors. Firstly, this was an era of freedom. All around the globe, enthused by Mahatma Gandhi's non-violence struggle for freedom of India, more and more countries had shaken off their foreign yoke. India's freedom in a sense marked the beginning of a period which saw the end of colonialism. Along with the spirit of freedom, a very strong nationalistic ideology influenced the economic decisions of these newly independent countries as well as of India. Secondly, in the case of India, Nehru and the Indian National Congress greatly influenced the shape of policy on the economic front. Nehru's leaning towards socialism was known and was clearly expressed. A band of intellectual freedom fighters along with Nehru were enthused by such socialistic zeal. The National Planning Committee of the Indian National Congress formed in 1938 was clearly marked by views, which were radical and clear. The planning proposal put forward by K.T. Shah, Secretary of the Committee states —

> "Private monopolies in key industries or services are dangerous, and must be rigorously forbidden... Public utilities ... should be conducted as public monopolies. New industries, suitable only for large-scale work by power-driven machinery and for standardized mass production, where no private vested interests now exist, must be established and conducted as public enterprise. All key industries must be State-owned and State-managed. The profit motive must be summarily and completely excluded from the conduct and organisation of every such industry. Where in any such key industry, private enterprise exists, and has created vested interests, these must be bought out, and the industry nationalized, subject to the payment of a just compensation... The foreign trade of the country must be a public monopoly, conducted as an integral part of the National Plan."[5]

Even as late as 1956, while speaking on India's Second Five Year Plan, Nehru made the following statement in the Lok Sabha :

> "I believe that ultimately all the principal means of production will be owned by the nation, but I just do not see why I should do something today which limits our progress simply to satisfy some theoretical urge. I have no doubt that at the present stage in India the private sector has a very important task to fulfil, provided always that it works within the confines laid down, and provided always that it does not lead to the creation of monopolies and other evils that the accummulation of wealth gives rise to. I think we have enough power in our laws to keep the private sector in check."[6]

Nehru, however, was a pragmatic philosopher statesman. In the same speech, he discouraged claim for nationalisation and prescribed a cautious role for the private sector.

This was also a time when some positive infrastructure development activities were taken up even though tourism had not yet developed as the dynamic industry that it is today. During this period, a Tourist Traffic Branch was set up in the Ministry of Transport of the Government of India. An Overseas Tourist Office was set up in New York in 1952. The Indian Airlines and Air-India started operating in 1953. The flagship Five-star hotel—Ashok—was built in the public sector and the India Tourism Development Corporation was formed in 1966.

(2) ***Nationalisations :*** The period from 1970 to 1984 was a period of nationalisations. This was a period in which the role of the private sector came to be recognised increasingly but still in a rather ad hoc manner and not as a matter of policy. Most States of India came up with various incentives and loans for development of transport and accommodation in the private sector. In 1982, the first Tourism Policy, as already mentioned, was formulated. The policy did not specify any clear role to the private sector, but did emphasise that tourism development was a 'joint effort' of all concerned. But all such pious ideas were overshadowed by a spate of nationalisation measures.

Some of the most important nationalisations started around 1969 but gained momentum after the popular electoral mandate for Mrs Indira Gandhi in 1971. Starting with the nationalisation of Suez Canal in Egypt, this was also a period in which in many places around the globe, ideology played a very strong part in economic planning. Ownership of means of production was seen as an important element in the efforts towards meeting the basic needs. In most places, as also in India, the period started with the nationalisation of raw materials and mineral sector. Oil industry, for example, played a very important role in the country's balance of payments. Industries which have very strong 'forward linkages' were important for operation of the national economy. Most of the countries embarking on national economic planning, during this period, therefore, found control of such enterprises essential. In India, the government carried out a series of nationalisations—the most important of them being nationalisation of 14 banks in 1969. In the same year, the Government enacted the Monopolies and Restrictive Trade Practices Act, 1969 and modified the Industrial Licensing Policy in 1970. The coal nationalisation took place in the early 1970s. By May, 1973, in a series of measures, the entire coal industry, except the coal mines attached to the private sector steel plants came under public ownership.

The Congress Party's manifesto for the 1971 General Elections had clearly set out the agenda for nationalisation, viz.—

> "The expansion of the public sector by taking over general insurance; increasing State participation in the import-export trade; greater role of the State in industries where substantial public funds have been invested; and expansion of the activities of the Food Corporation of India, coordinated with cooperatives, which can ensure the implementation of a national policy for the distribution of food and fair prices for the farmers."[7]

In May, 1971, management of 106 general insurance companies was taken over by an Ordinance and they were nationalised in August, 1972 completing the process started with nationalisation of life insurance in 1956. The wholesale wheat trading was nationalised in 1973 marking the culmination of the march to ownership of means of production having already in 1972 nationalised the steel giant Indian Iron and Steel Company and cotton textile mills between 1972 and 1976.

(3) ***Partnerships :*** The period from 1984 to 1991 can be considered to be the first phase of partnership between the public and private sectors.

A new approach to economic philosophy where the private sector plays a dynamic role started emerging during this period and the Five Year Plans of this period reflected this change in approach. Many State Governments declared tourism as an 'industry'. The National Committee on Tourism made many recommendations highlighting the role of the private sector and also recommended measures for achieving such collaboration. The Report recommended the formation of a National Tourism Board, the establishment of a Tourism Finance Corporation of India, joint marketing with the private sector and package of incentives for private enterprise. These ideas coming from the National Committee started a process of rethinking and debate which were to germinate later on into concrete ideas.

Though the process of liberalisation was started in 1984, clearly its time had not yet come. The process could not be carried out fully, partly because the hegemony of socialistic ideas continued to cast a shadow over liberalisation ideas and Marxist ideology inherent in the political system continued to restrain any move towards liberalisation.

(4) ***Liberalisation:*** 1991 marked the beginning of a new period of economic liberalisation, and of wide economic reforms based on the role of the market in determining the parameters of economic activities. Private initiative and participation became the catchword for development. Numerous steps taken to liberalise the economy resulted in greater competitiveness. Measures to encourage both foreign and domestic private investment in areas earlier reserved for the public sector created great enthusiasm all round, generated new confidence in the strength of the economy and emphasised India's new role as one of the emerging economies of the 21st Century. The tourism sector, primarily driven by private enterprise as it is, expected this new atmosphere to provide a new fillip. There is, however, a widely shared feeling in the tourism sector that this new partnership has not yet taken place.

Today, in India there is an atmosphere responsive to the idea of partnership. There is need for the private sector to play a dynamic role in the development of tourism. The government has to provide the regulatory framework to enable the private sector to play that role. There is scope for much more action than seen so far, from both the sides.

References

1. Inaugural address of Prime Minister Shri Atal Behari Vajpayee at the National Conference and Annual Session of the Confederation of Indian Industries (CII) on 28th April, 1998.
2. Seventh Five Year Plan—Planning Commission of India, Vol. II, p. 234.
3. Eighth Five Year Plan—Planning Commission of India, Vol. II, pp. 253-54.
4. Draft National Tourism Policy—Department of Tourism, 1997, (mimeograph).
5. Nayar, Baldev Raj : India's Mixed Economy- p.158, Popular Prakashan Private Limited, Bombay. 1989.
6. Nayar, *op. cit.*, p. 203.
7. Nayar : *op. cit.* p. 297.

5

Sustainable Tourism

In 1855, President Franklin Pierce of the United States made a 'request' to Chief Sealth of the Suwanish tribe of American Indians, who live in what is now the State of Washington, to 'sell' his land to the Government. In reply, Chief Sealth sent the following letter to the President :

"How can you buy or sell the sky, the warmth of the land? The idea is strange to us. Yet we do not own the freshness of the air or the sparkle of the water. How can you buy them from us? Every part of this earth is sacred to my people. Every shining pine needle, every sandy shore, every mist in the dark woods, every clearing and humming insect is holy in the memory and experience of my people..."

"...And what is there to life if a man cannot hear the lovely cry of the whippoorwill or the argument of the frogs around a pond at night? The Red Indian prefers the soft sound of the wind itself cleaned by the midnight rain, or scented with a pine. The air is precious to the Red man, for all things share the same breath—the beasts, the trees, the man. The White man does not seem to notice the air he breathes. Like a man dying for many years, he is numbed to the smell...

When the last Red man has vanished from the earth, and the memory is only the shadow of a cloud moving across the prairie, these shores and forests will still hold the spirits of my people."

The World Commission on Environment and Development defines 'sustainable development' as "development that meets the needs of the

---

This chapter is based on an official presentation made by the author in W.T.O. Conference on 'Sustainable Tourism Development' in the Maldives in February, 1997.

present without compromising the ability of future generations to meet their own needs". Since the 1992 Earth Summit, the concept of 'sustainable development' has been placed firmly on the global agenda and this issue is assuming great significance in the development of tourism.

There are basically three principles of sustainable development. These principles are equally applicable to tourism development as well. Firstly, development must be ecologically sustainable, i.e., the ecological processes must not be adversely affected. Secondly, social and cultural sustainability — which means that tourism development is compatible with the culture and values of the local people and that the basic cultural identity of the community is not adversely affected. Thirdly, development must be economically sustainable in a process which allows such development to take place in an efficient management of resources. Such management must ensure that the resources can support the future as well as the current generations.

Unfortunately, quite often, the negative aspects of tourism development get highlighted whereas the benefits which flow directly or indirectly are not noticed. The WTO Publication — Sustainable Tourism Development : Guide for Local Planners (by George McIntyre) has summed up a model form of sustainable tourism as one designed to —

(a) improve the quality of life of the people;
(b) provide a good experience to the tourists; and
(c) maintain the quality of environment which is essential for both the tourists and local community.

The benefits of sustainable tourism has been summed up very adequately as follows :—

- "Sustainable tourism encourages an understanding of the impacts of tourism on the natural, cultural, and human environments.
- Sustainable tourism ensures a fair distribution of benefits and costs.
- Tourism generates local employment, both directly in the tourism sector and in various support and resource management sectors.
- Tourism stimulates profitable domestic industries — hotels and other lodging facilities, restaurants and other food services, transportation systems, handicrafts, and guide services.

- Tourism generates foreign exchange for the country and injects capital and the new money into the local economy.
- Tourism diversifies the local economy, particularly in rural areas where agricultural employment may be sporadic or insufficient.
- Sustainable tourism seeks decision-making among all segments of the society, including local populations, so that tourism and other resource users can coexist. It incorporates planning and zoning which ensure tourism development appropriate to the carrying capacity of the ecosytem.
- Tourism stimulates improvements to local transportation, communications, and other basic community infrastructures.
- Tourism creates recreational facilities which can be used by local communities as well as domestic and international visitors. It also encourages and helps pay for preservation of archaeological sites, and historic buildings and districts.
- Nature tourism encourages productive use of lands which are marginal for agriculture, enabling large tracts to remain covered in natural vegetation.
- Cultural tourism enhances local community esteem and provides the opportunity for greater understanding and communication among peoples of diverse backgrounds.
- Environmentally sustainable tourism demonstrates the importance of natural and cultural resources to a community's economic and social well-being and can help to preserve them.
- Sustainable tourism monitors, assesses and manages the impacts of tourism, develops reliable methods of environmental accountability, and counters any negative effect."[1]

The inter-relation between the benefits of sustainable tourism, the responsibility of the Government and the local community is demonstrated in the following illustration-

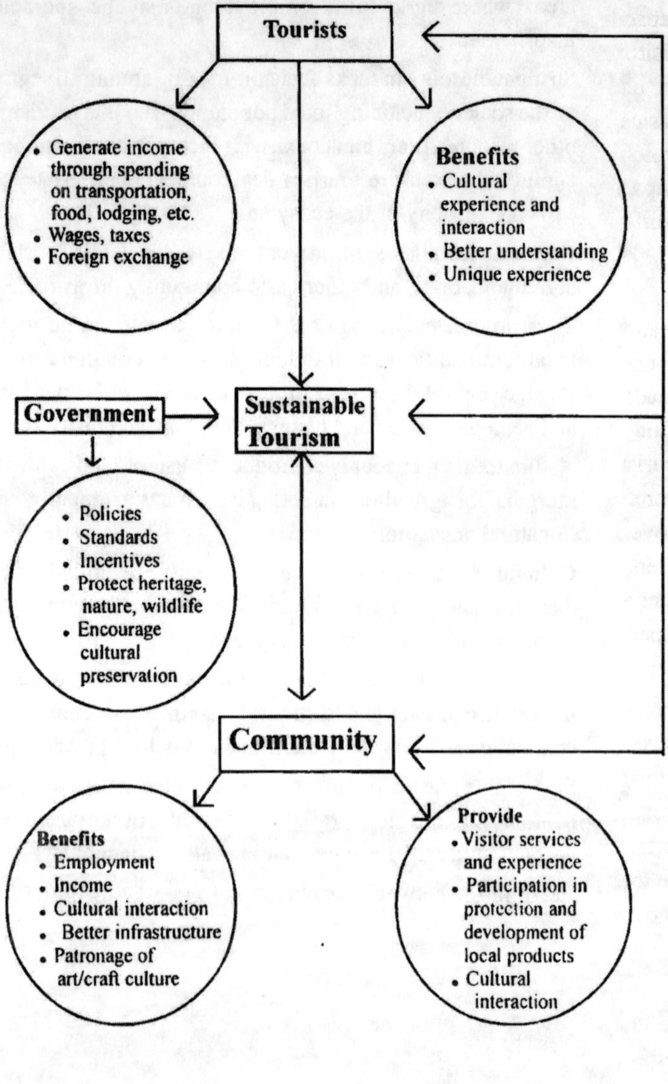

With the help of —

WTO : Sustainable Tourism Development, 1993 —pp. 6-23.

It is obvious that in any sustainable tourism planning, the environment, the ecology and the community are the key considerations. In planning sustainable tourism, therefore, an awareness about what is commonly referred to as the carrying capacity is of fundamental importance. Carrying capacity which covers ecological relationship, socio-cultural impact, and visitor experience cannot always be adequately quantified but nevertheless an understanding of the same is of importance. Carrying capacity basically refers to an assessment of the maximum use of any tourism site which does not cause tension for the host community and avoids adverse impact on the resources and on the psychological satisfaction of the tourists.

Conflicts, however, are inherent in the very process of tourism development. The issues which may cause such tensions have been beautifully examined in the background paper "The Social Impacts of Tourism" prepared by Professor C.L. Jenkins for the World Tourism Leaders Meeting on Social Impacts of Tourism in Manila, Philippines on 22nd May, 1997.[2] For the tour operators and travel agents who sell the tourism products, it is primarily a commercial proposition. There is, therefore, an inherent potential of conflict between what sells and what the Government and local agencies would like to project. Prof. Jenkins also refers to cultural stress caused by what is called 'demonstration effect'. Such effect results from transferring to the host community, examples and experiences of different cultures and lifestyles and also of different income levels which brings a sense of exploitation to the local community.

But Prof. Jenkins has shown that cultural deterioration need not be caused by tourism development alone and not even by tourism development primarily. Such changes are influenced by many factors including economic factors. To what extent a society can insulate itself against such deterioration will depend on the awareness generated in the community, the Government policy towards protection and the willingness of those who are affected to take steps for such protection, and also on the inherent strength of the social fabric itself.

An adverse impact of tourism could also be in relation to the stress that the local systems have to undergo as a result of the large inflow of the tourists. Unless tourism is properly and carefully planned, greater pressure from visitors can cause what is called "*irridex effect*" — causing irritation to the local people because they are deprived of the basic civic amenities which are diverted for the benefit of the tourists. Tourism growth may change the rhythm of a community's lifestyle.

In most cases, all such effects are possible but they need not necessarily be present in all cases. Quite often, such tension arises out of a tourist's lack of knowledge of the local culture and tradition and the weakness of the local system in handling the same.

The agenda for action, therefore, should concentrate around community participation in tourism development and planning, training of the personnel associated with tourism development so that they can provide quality services without devaluing the same. In the framework of action it is necessary to ensure that the benefits to the community are so spread out that the people perceive the benefits flowing to them. Similarly, there is need for a legal and procedural framework that deals adequately with social evils like exploitation, child abuse, sex tourism, interference with heritage products, etc.

Tourism can provide immense benefits and can be a tool for protection and preservation of the heritage of the country. Instead of being seen as an irritant to sustainable development, a little initiative from the planners can make tourism the vehicle for preservation of ecology and heritage. Harping on the negative aspect only could be self-defeating academic dogmatism not in tune with the future aspirations and requirements of mankind.

The National Tourism Policy, 1982 emphasised the importance of a judicious balance between conservation and development. "A major consideration of tourism development," the Policy states, "will be to preserve our culture and natural heritage which constitutes the major tourism resource of the country"[3]. Since then, however, major changes have taken place in the socio-economic and political situation in India and the global geo-political realities have also undergone tremendous changes. The country is now launching its Ninth Five Year Plan. In the beginning of this decade, India also embarked on a major policy of economic reforms and liberalisation and moved away from the rigours of quantitative controls of planned economic development to a liberalised, reformed and market-driven economic regime. In the changed scenario, the Government is having a new look at the Tourism Policy. The published draft of the new policy has—

(i) placed tourism as a central input in the economic development process because of its role in resource generation and employment creation;

(ii) focussed on the role of tourism in socio-economic development of the backward areas, weaker sections, women and artisans;

(iii) allowed these goals to be pursued in tune with the goal of the enrichment of the environment and the ecosystem; and

(iv) recognised the role of tourism as a potent global force for national and international understanding and for creating awareness for sustainable development.[4]

Any policy for sustainable development will naturally revolve around the following cardinal principles,—

(a) that there is need for striking a balance between development and conservation;

(b) that there is need for commitment of the nation as a whole to the goals of sustainable tourism development;

(c) that adequate, effective and pragmatic control systems are devised and are efficiently put into place; and

(d) that the policy incorporates and motivates cooperation of the local community who must perceive the benefit of such participation and should be able to partake the same.

India is fortunate and unique in having such geographical diversity that has given it a wealth of ecosystems which are well protected and preserved. These ecosystems have become the major resources for eco-tourism in India. These consist of, —

—biosphere reserves;

—mangroves;

—corals and coral reefs;

—deserts;

—mountains and forests;

—flora and fauna; and

—sea, lakes and rivers.

The policy objectives mentioned above particularly in the context of ecotourism can be achieved only by a process of selective approach, scientific planning, effective control and continuous monitoring. The

Government policy on tourism has shown, at least theoretically, sensitivity to the environmental concerns. The Tourism Policy of 1982 and guidelines on ecotourism aim to achieve some of the following objectives, that, —

(a) the level of development is compatible with the general capacity of the physical environment and resources;

(b) sufficient facilities and services are provided to serve the tourists and the local population;

(c) the hotel rooms are distributed in such a manner that the natural characteristics and qualities of the area are enhanced;

(d) the tourism-related constructions are designed carefully and sensitively to merge with the surroundings to enhance the natural beauty; and

(e) the architectural heritage sites and other areas of historic value are protected adequately.

In the initial years of the development of ecotourism, greater emphasis was laid on the development of the Himalayas and the deserts in the State of Rajasthan . The mighty Himalayas encircling India in the north not only provide immensely diverse tourism attractions but also influence the climate, rainfall and the flow of rivers in India. Ecotourism in the Himalayan region, therefore, is the basic corner stone of ecotourism policy in India.

The Himalayan Tourism Advisory Board (HIMTAB) was set up by the Government of India in 1987 as a voluntary consultative mechanism for mutual cooperation between the States in Himalayan region to promote integrated tourism. The Board meets at different places in the Himalayan States and formulates policies and programmes for the development of tourism in the region. The issues considered by the Board in various meetings so far include development of alternate resorts to reduce over-crowding in the established tourist spots, use of alternate sources of energy, registration of porters and guides and their training and motivation, coordination of mountain rescue operations, preservation of ecosystem, establishment of effective communication, efficient garbage disposal systems, safety and security of tourists, etc.

It is recognised that as a first step in the development of tourism, haphazard growth has to be checked and a future strategy has to be properly planned. India being a federal polity composed of many States and Union Territories, the idea of a National Master Plan is not a feasible one. At the national level, therefore, an attempt is made to collate the Master Plans of the States and to coordinate the activities of different States in tune with the national policy of sustainable development.

In addition, to ensure that environmental and ecological needs are carefully nurtured and that in the name of tourism development, the fragile ecosystem is not exploited in too many small schemes, a strategy of 'Special Tourism Area' has been devised by the Government of India. Under this scheme, the State Governments are required to identify and notify suitable areas as 'Special Tourism Area' so that comprehensive development plans for such areas can be taken up. The identification of such areas is done on the basis of its tourism potential and the ability to attract private investment for its development on a commercial basis. The Government's involvement in such Special Tourism Areas should be only to the extent of providing the basic infrastructural development. The States of Kerala, Orissa and Maharashtra have developed such Special Tourism Areas.

Currently, the Government of India is encouraging various forms of tourism which have direct impact on preservation of heritage and culture; developing Heritage Railway Tourism in Rajasthan, Gujarat and Darjeeling; creation of amusement parks, science cities, and providing an impetus to the promotion of industrial tourism, are but a few steps in this direction. Fairs like "Suraj Kund Mela" based on the concept of craft and ethnicity have been big draws with the tourists. The Government of India's assistance for promoting local initiative through regional fairs and festivals not only provides for growth of tourism through economic impetus for the local community, but also facilitates inter-regional interaction within the country.

Regulations and Sustainability

While the major emphasis in the development of sustainable tourism is on public participation and involvement, it is essential that the Government plays the role of coordinating and controlling the activities to arrive at the objectives defined. Alive to this requirement, a number of regulations have already been put into place by the Government of India.

Many of these legislations are designed to protect ecologically fragile and sensitive ecosystems. Some of the important ones among them are:

(i) Forest (Conservation) Act, 1980 which controls the use of forests for non-forestry uses.

(ii) Wildlife (Protection) Act, 1972 which designates the National Parks and Wildlife Sanctuaries and stipulates a comprehensive framework for wildlife protection and conservation.

(iii) Environment Protection Act, 1986 stipulates several measures for protecting and improving the quality of the environment and preventing, controlling and abating environmental pollution. Coastal Regulation Zones (CRZ) were gazetted by a notification under the Act in 1991 and a wide range of activities have been prohibited in the sea coast within 500 metres of High Tide Line (HTL).

Guidelines for Ecotourism

In addition to the above regulations, recently the Government of India have worked out certain broad guidelines for ecotourism which stipulate that the developmental process itself should meet the following cardinal principles—

(i) It should involve the local community and lead to the overall economic development of the area.

(ii) It should identify areas where conflicts may arise because the resource used for promotion of tourism may be the same from which local community get their livelihood. Ecotourism policy attempts to minimize such conflicts by finding ways to balance needs for development with necessity of preservation.

(iii) The type and scale of tourism development should be compatible with the environment and socio-cultural characteristics of the local community.

(iv) Ecotourism policy should be planned as a part of the overall area development strategy and should be guided by an integrated land use plan. It should not be seen as something alien to environment.

The guidelines for ecotourism development planning also cover many other important issues. Some of the salient features can be briefly mentioned as :

(a) Decisions for the development of tourism in ecologically fragile areas have to be based on a thorough understanding of local resources, social and economic factors and other characteristics. The objectives of tourism development in any specific area as well as the intended beneficiaries, have to be decided on the basis of these factors and on the strength of discussions and negotiations with those most directly concerned.

(b) The development of physical infrastructure for tourism should be preceded by the preparation of an inventory of the available resources and a careful zoning/management plan to ensure proper use and preservation of valuable natural sites.

(c) Wherever for tourism development, destruction or serious alteration of areas of high primary productivity like wetland, seagrass beds, coral reefs, rain forests becomes necessary, eareful social and economic cost-benefit analysis should precede any such planning. Further, planning and promotion of tourism should be undertaken as a component part of an integrated, comprehensive resource management plan based on sound ecological principles.

(d) The 'Tourism Management Plan' should also establish standards for resort development, covering among others, the style and locations of structures, treatment of sewage and control of litter, preservation of open spaces and public use of fragile areas. It should further lay down procedures to ensure that sewage is not directed to the beach and that the groundwater and solid waste like litter, garbage, trash, etc., are systematically collected and disposed suitably. The planning and regulatory process should carefully go into various details that have bearing on the ecology and should specify methods for construction materials to be used for such construction, encourage use of eco-friendly local materials, minimise noise pollution, etc.

(e) Physical planning and design should integrate community services, transportation and tourism. There are numerous instances of community life style being adversely affected and hardship caused to them because of pressure on limited civic amenities when influx of tourists takes place without proper planning for civic services, transportation, etc.

Ecology and Tourism: A Vision of the Future

It would be pertinent to ponder over what the global community and the Government of India can do to ensure that the rich inheritance is enhanced and enriched and passed on to the future generation instead of being debased and eroded in mindless commercial exploitation. Indian tourism today is based primarily on either the gift of nature or what history has bestowed over thousands of years. In a developing country like India, with such tremendous pressure of population, there is eagerness and struggle for economic betterment as quickly as possible. Tourism provides many avenues for quick earnings. For a national policy, there cannot be any two opinions about preserving the surroundings for the benefit of the present and the future generations. But for many engaged in daily struggle for survival, considerations of today's earnings take precedence over thoughts for tomorrows's heritage. They would find much philosophical truth in the famous statement of Lord Keynes that "in the long run we are all dead". One of the greatest challenges for tourism planning today, therefore, is to achieve that amount of public motivation where exploitation of the environment and ecosystem do not exceed the accepted optimal level of carrying capacity. There is, therefore, an urgency in dovetailing the short-term gains from tourism exploitation of the ecosystem with the long-term compulsions of maintaining the ecosystem. Conscious and serious efforts, therefore, will have to be made to find a balance between these two conflicting trends and to take concrete steps to preserve the heritage which is not renewable.

There is already consciousness all around the globe on these issues. This consciousness perhaps needs to be developed into a common durable vision and to evolve some ideology to pursue. It is perhaps necessary to create a movement to spread the ideologies and to take them beyond the realm of usual declarations of intent. Perhaps the 600 million tourists that go round the globe annually today — and that number is swelling — be made the ambassadors of such a global movement for creating awareness for a sustainable tourism development.

Most developing countries face the dilemma that the absolute cost of protecting the socio-cultural and ecological environment is too high and at the same time the cost of not developing such heritage for economic use also is too high to ignore. Even to translate the nation's honest intentions regarding eco-friendly tourism into action, trained manpower, pool of experts and professionals are needed whose services can be used to blend the economic needs with sustainable development. Many nations do not have the resources to acquire such expertise.

Naturally serious sustainable development movements would also need resources and most nations who need such movements do not have such resources. Lord Keynes had the vision to mastermind the creation, out of the despair of the war ravaged world of two institutions—the World Bank and the International Monetary Fund (IMF)—which continue to provide hope and ideas to the world. Before our inheritance on which tourism revolves run the risk of irreparable damage, it is time to think of such an international organisation which can not only provide the ideology but also would be instrumental in providing resources to shape that ideology into a meaningful action plan.

All across the globe, there are millions of people who still share such ideas and would be willing to join hands in making such a vision a reality. India can make a beginning in this regard.

References

1. Sustainable Tourism Development: Guide for Local Planners (by George McIntyre) WTO, Madrid, 1993.
2. C.L. Jenkins : The Social Impact of Tourism in WTO - World Tourism Leaders Meeting on Social Impacts of Tourism, May, 1997.
3. Tourism Policy, 1982, p. 14.
4. Draft National Tourism Policy, 1997.

6

International and Regional Cooperation

The World Tourism Organization (WTO)

"As tourism grew and became an integral part of the fabric of modern life", says the White Paper on the Future of the Organization, prepared by the World Tourism Organisation,[1] "its international dimension increased and States started to play an increasingly important role — their activities covering the whole spectrum from infrastructure to regulations." Along with the growing importance of tourism and its emergence as an industry of the future, and greater growth potentials projected for the 21st century, the nature and mechanism of inter-governmental cooperation have undergone changes. Many of the issues likely to shape the future are global in their impact. Today, the World Tourism Organization as the nodal agency entrusted by the United Nations with the promotion and development of tourism plays a key role in shaping that future. With 138 countries and territories as its members *(Appendix-IV)* and more than 350 affiliate members representing various sectors of tourism industry, the WTO is a key institution in translating the objectives of tourism for development and promotion of understanding across the globe.

It is, however, significant that the beginning of the WTO was not as an inter-governmental agency. It started as the International Union of Official Tourist Publicity Organizations set up in 1925 in The Hague. After the World War II, it moved to Geneva and came to be known as International Union for Official Tourism Organizations (IUOTO). It was a technical non-governmental organization but had substantial membership of international tourism organizations and in the initial years had been an important channel for piloting the directions of tourism growth. But, as mentioned earlier, by the, '60s, tourism had expanded to touch various aspects of human life and naturally the Governments started playing an increasingly important role in regulation and control. It was felt, therefore, that the organizational pattern was in need of change. In 1969, a resolution was moved in the United Nations General Assembly to transform it into an inter-governmental organization to function in cooperation with the other existing machinery within the United Nations. In 1975, the IUOTO was renamed as the World Tourism Organization and its first General Assembly was held in Madrid in May, 1975. In 1976, the WTO became an executive agency of the United Nations Development Programme (UNDP) and in 1977, by a formal cooperation agreement, it became part of the United Nations itself.

The General Assembly is the supreme organ of the structure of WTO. The Executive Council is the Governing Board of the WTO for monitoring its activities and regulating the budget. The activities of the WTO are carried out through six Regional Commissions — Africa, the Americas, East Asia and the Pacific, Europe, the Middle East and South Asia. In addition, there are specialized committees to advise the WTO on special programme contents. WTO is primarily financed by members' contributions.

Objectives of the WTO

The WTO's Statute laid down the following primary objectives for the Organization :-

(1) "The fundamental aim of the organization shall be the promotion and development of tourism with a view to contributing to economic development, international understanding, peace, prosperity, and universal respect for, and observance of, human rights and fundamental freedoms for all without distinction as to race, sex, language or religion. The organization shall take all appropriate action to attain this objective.

(2) In pursuing this aim, the organization shall pay particular attention to the interests of the developing countries in the field of tourism.

(3) In order to establish its central role in the field of tourism, the Organization shall establish and maintain effective collaboration with the appropriate organs of the United Nations and its

specialized agencies. In this connection, the organization shall seek a cooperative relationship with and a participation in the activities of the United Nations Development Programme (UNDP), as a participating and executing agency."[2]

The WTO, through its activities, helps the nations throughout the world to maximise the positive impacts of tourism and also to create an appropriate opinion and awareness for sustainable development of tourism. The primary activities of the WTO revolve around its basic objectives and are specifically grouped into the following six broad areas : -

- Cooperation for Development
- Statistics, Economic Analysis and Market Research
- Environment, Planning and Finance
- Quality of Tourism Development
- Human Resource Development
- Communications and Documentation

During the last thirty years, the WTO has initiated a number of steps in each of these areas. Involving the member states and other organizations, on the objectives of sustainable tourism, the WTO has succeeded in adopting a whole set of Declarations on all aspects of tourism development *(Appendix-V)*. All these Declarations have helped the nations of the world to think about the key issues confronting them and aim to create public opinion and the commitment of the nations to address those issues. Similarly, the WTO's initiatives on statistics and market research have helped in bringing into sharp focus the benefits of tourism. It has also developed standard procedures and key parameters for properly documenting such impact.

Today, as tourism grows and the frontiers of activities ever increase, the WTO also faces new challenges. The changing market environment, the decreasing role of national tourism authorities and decentralization as well as decreasing role of the Central Government in many federal structures, have made it necessary for the WTO to look at new structures and alternative models of cooperation. The emergence of such forces and the resultant withdrawal of important countries like USA, Canada and Belgium from the WTO have not only affected the resources of the Organization but also made it necessary to re-examine its role and its organizational structure. While the WTO tries to brace itself up, to meet the new challenges and tries to be in tune with the demands of market forces, it is also faced with a dilemma. It cannot forsake the developing nations who require the benefits of tourism most and who are least equipped to protect themselves from the market forces unless organizations like the WTO come to their assistance. Faced with such a dilemma, the WTO is increasingly trying to evolve a new structure that allows for closer public-private collaboration.

India has been a member of the organization right from its inception and has the privilege of being in the Executive Council for a number of years. India, therefore, takes a pride of place in shaping the future of the international organization on tourism. As has been shown elsewhere, the WTO has done some extremely valuable work to assess the existing market trends and to evaluate the forces that will influence the nature and direction of growth in future. It has also projected the likely growth of tourism in different countries. These inputs are of invaluable assistance to policy makers and planners.

The analysis of these trends and the lessons to be drawn from them, form the core of this book also.

Regional Cooperation in South Asia

While talking of regional cooperation, the concept of a region changes depending on the perception or depending on particular relevance of the sector for which such cooperation is talked about. In tourism, India's concern for regional cooperation has most prominently been in relation to South Asia. Such preoccupation primarily flows from geographical proximity, a sense of physical homogenenty, and cultural affinity. The urge and wherewithal for operational initiatives for such cooperation comes from the political and economic drive behind the spirit of the South Asian Association for Regional Cooperation (SAARC). However, other common interests have led to emergence of regional cooperation in tourism not always influenced by geographical proximity. Pacific Asia Travel Association (PATA), Indian Ocean Rim Travel Agents Association, BIMST-EC (Bangladesh India, Myanmar, Srilanka, Thailand-Economic Coorperation) are examples of other attempts to explore ways of cooperation between countries and organizations sharing common objectives. Regional cooperation in tourism in South Asia, however, dominates the thinking.

The South Asia region is a huge geographical mass and is the home to about 1/5th of the total world population. The great tourism boom has also affected this region but the share of the region in the total arrivals is a meagre 0.7 per cent. India dominates the scene with a share of 51.5 per cent of the arrivals and 74.5 per cent of the earnings. The region has tremendous potentials, and wide variety of tourist attractions, often unmatched.

The question can reasonably be asked "Why should South Asia look to tourism as a means of socio-economic development?" Firstly, South Asia region needs to have a closer look at tourism because today, South Asia perhaps needs a push more than any other region to get out of the vicious cycle of poverty. The Human Development Report of 1997 reported that two-fifths of the total of 1.3 billion estimated income poor, i.e. 515 million people are below dollar a day poverty line in South Asia. And, in spite of tremendous progress made by the region, in various human development indicators, the per capital GNP in East Asia and the Pacific region is 18 times that of South Asia.

The second simple answer to the question perhaps will take us back to the classical economic theory of 'comparative advantage'. The region has comparative advantage over many other places in the world in terms of nature's endowments and the richness of cultural and historical heritage. It would be appropriate, therefore, to exploit this advantage for the benefit of the common man rather than try to follow development prescriptions relevant to other situations.

In the South Asian context, while replying to the general question 'Why Tourism', it is again relevant to refer to the very significant experience of Mexico as related by the former Secretary General of World Tourism Organisation and the former Minister (Planning and Finance) in Mexico, Mr Antonio Savignac and quoted elsewhere. All those reasons which make tourism an important tool of socio-economic development, are relevant in the regional context.

The question can certainly be asked. 'Is the Mexican experience relevant for South Asia?' What are the potentials for tourism development in South Asia? Again, the future projections arrived at by the World Tourism and Travel Council[3] could make the policy planners in the region sit up and take notice. Just a few samples of the forecast :

- In South Asia, travel and tourism is expected to generate US$ 44.4 billion of economic activity and 33.7 million jobs in 1998. By 2010, South Asia travel and tourism is expected to produce US$ 169.6 billion of economic activity and 57.8 million jobs.
- The South Asia travel and tourism economy is expected to contribute 8.6 per cent to Gross Domestic Product in 1998. By 2010 this contribution should increase to 11.8 per cent.
- In South Asia, employment (direct and indirect), resulting from the travel and tourism economy is expected to total 7.8 per cent in 1998, or 1 in every 12.9 jobs. By 2010, this total should grow to 10.5 per cent or 1 in every 9.5 jobs.
- In South Asia, travel and tourism exports make up an important share of travel and tourism's contribution to Gross Domestic Product. Of total exports, services and merchandise, travel and tourism is expected to generate 11.0 per cent in 1998, growing to 12.5 per cent by 2010.
- Total taxes from travel and tourism in South Asia in 1998 are expected to total US$ 9.8 billion or 8.3 per cent of total, while it expected to benefit from US$ 2.1 billion, or 5.1 per cent of total government operating expenditures. Over the next 12 years, South Asia travel and tourism taxes are expected to grow to US$ 36.0 billion or 10.9 per cent of total taxes. In contrast, government spending is forecast to grow to US$ 6.8 billion, or 6.5 per cent of overall government spending.

Unfortunately, if we look at the WTO statistics of tourism in the economy of the South Asia, the position does not emerge as so encouraging. Tourism receipts is only 0.1 per cent of the GNP in Bangladesh, 1.7 per cent in Bhutan, 0.9 per cent in India, 0.2 per cent in Pakistan, 1.8 per cent in Sri Lanka. Similarly, tourism receipts as percentage of merchandise exports is only 0.7 per cent in Bangladesh, 9 per cent in India, 1.4 per cent in Pakistan and 5.9 per cent in Sri Lanka. Maldives has a very high percentage, both in GNP and in merchandise exports but then Maldives' special position does not fully explain the South Asia position.

Why tourism has not played a more significant role in the economic activities of the region? It appears in the South Asian countries, awareness about the importance of tourism is not at the most desirable level nor has tourism been placed at the level of priority it deserves. While such awareness is low in the individual countries, in the overall socio-economic scenario, even as a group, the region has not shown such awareness. In the institutional and organizational set up of SAARC, tourism does not seen to have a visible presence.

Any future planning for the region can be based only on the availability of adequate and comprehensive statistics. Unfortunately, it appears that the basic information for South Asia region as a whole is not available, not even in the SAARC Secretariat. My effort to get such information about the contribution of tourism to employment generation in South Asia elicited only a negative response. Therefore, the plan of action for any regional cooperation must be built on three fundamental requirements. First, an awareness about the role of tourism in general and the commitment of the government as whole in each country and of all the countries together as a region, to the spirit of regional co-operation. Secondly building a good regional organisational base to focus on the issues of tourism and, thirdly, developing a strong statistical base for the region as a whole and establishing linkages for information flows.

The WTO projection for growth of tourism regionwise till 2020 can sometimes lead the South Asia region to a false sense of complacency. South Asia is expected to grow at the rate of 6.1 per cent which is higher than the projected growth rate of the world as a whole. However, even if this projection comes true, the total share of the South Asia in the world arrivals will be only 1.2 per cent by 2020.

But, the more important point is that this growth rate will not be possible unless positive efforts are made, to overcome the infrastructure bottlenecks, to take up dynamic and professional marketing and to train human resources to provide the required quality in services. We have also to keep in mind the emerging trends in the world and to fashion out our strategy to be in tune with those trends. The tourism market trends brought out by the WTO have shown that the region depends heavily on Europe, the market share of which has grown to 43 per cent by 1997. The region has, therefore, to carefully watch the implications of the emergence of the Euro currency and of the European Union. The other important implication for South Asia presently is the impact of the Asian financial crises. It has been estimated that the impact may be two-fold. Firstly, the outbound tourism from the East Asia and the Pacific region will decline till about the year 2000 and South Asia may lose about 150,000 arrivals because of this decline. On the other hand, the East Asia and the Pacific region has become a better value for money to tourists from long-haul regions. It is estimated that by the year 2000, such attractions for East Asia and the Pacific would cost about 175,000 arrivals to the South Asia region.[3]

Such a brief look at the scenario, as outlined above, also indicates the various areas in which action need to be taken. Some of these areas can be summed up as follows :-

- First, the region has to realise that its development can't be in a static situation nor in isolation. Its planning and strategies must be capable of responding to the fast changing situations and must be in tune with the emerging trends. When competition is so acute, the standards achieved must be the best. At present, the region is not equipped properly for such response.
- Second, the one point agenda should be to get away from generalities to specifics. Leaving aside the gradiose ideas for the time being, it is necessary to identify few simple solutions and action points, and to implement them, and monitor regularly.
- The South Asia region can be projected as a compact destination, each country supplementing and enhancing the attractions of the other so that the tourists get the best value for their money in planning a trip to the region as a whole. Therefore, there are tremendous opportunities for joint promotion and development of a marketing network, involving the private sector, and in particular, the tour operators and the travel agents.
- A closer interaction between the South Asian nations on tourism will allow it to have greater bargaining strength in various international organisations and in getting increasingly larger share of facilities available for the region from such international bodies. The South Asia region must have a potent common platform including the private sector to project it as a region in all fora where tourism is discussed.
- The region has different level of expertise in human resource development relating to tourism. A joint effort could benefit all the countries. The recent experience of the European Commission's sponsored Training of Trainers' Programme shows that such

regional co-operation could be quite effective. The termination of this scheme, in spite of its impact and in spite of the combined protest of the region, also shows that the bargaining strength of the region as a whole has not yet fully matured.

The Economic and Social Commission for Asia and the Pacific (ESCAP) has already taken up same initiatives in this regard which can provide the framework for future action. The promotion of regional cooperation in human resource development has been planned through a network of Asia-Pacific Education and Training Institutes in Tourism (APETIT). This networking is being conceived around five general activity groups.[4]

(a) Information management, through internet and database system.
(b) Communication links, through electronic newsletter, etc.
(c) Training and advisory services, sharing of training and educational facilities.
(d) Sharing of experience.
(e) Research and development, related to transfer of technology, joint research, training of trainers, etc.

- Even if the overall scenario is marked by some amount of contact at the government level between the countries of South Asia, the concept of public-private collaboration or partnership has not yet taken root in the region. Tourism being primarily a private sector driven initiative, development of a strong and dynamic private initiative in each country linked together in the region, would go a long way in strengthening the tourism promotion efforts.
- The WTO studies have shown that the future tourism trends will be influenced primarily by great developments in technologies. Technological collaboration and linkages would be the basis for any joint promotion activities that can be considered. Such linkages should be established between the SAARC Secretariat and the member nations as well as with the private sector organisations.
- Similarly, the tremendous growth in tourist traffic would also imply great expansion of air traffic in the region. Development of adequate air safety norms and collaboration between the countries of the region for providing the best communication facilities would strengthen the image of the region as a whole.

- Though intra-regional tourism in projected to decline in the future, for South Asia intra-regional tourism will continue to be the essence of tourism development and the spirit of regional tourism. All the countries must work towards removing all the bottlenecks to such intra-regional movements. The tourism policy of India has always emphasized the role of tourism in spreading international understanding and unity. The South Asia region needs this bond of understanding more than ever before.
- Both the public and private sector in the South Asia region must look at new markets. Long haul arrivals — 76 per cent - dominate South Asia tourism — whereas in most other areas inter-regional tourism has been prominent. Market diversification, greater attention to the emerging outbound markets of Asia-Pacific, should be a conscious regional policy. In many areas, like Buddhist pilgrimage, the region has ready common ground.

The spirit of regional tourism in South Asia is not a question of potential, nor of possibilities, not even of capabilities. It is primarily a question of the will to do something.

References

1. WTO : Adapting to Change — A World Tourism Organization for the 21st. Century, July, 1997.
2. WTO : Adapting to change op. cit. p. 4.
3. Tourism Market Trends : South Asia, 1998, WTO, p. 57.
4. ESCAP Perspective on Tourism Development in BIMST-EC Countries and its Role in Promoting Regional Cooperation. Paper presented at the conference on the BIMST-EC Strategy for Partnership in Tourism, Calcutta, 30-31 October, 1998 (Unpublished).

7

The Future Vision

"Would you tell me, please,
Which way I ought to walk from here?"
"That depends a good deal
on where you want to get to,
said the Cat."
Lewis Carroll "Alice's Adventures in Wonderland"

At a time when the country is joyously celebrating the 50th year of its independence and achievements as a free nation, it will be inappropriate to suggest that there is need to reassess the directions of our progress. Yet in the case of tourism one does feel that while the progress has been substantial, much of it has been achieved without a conscious direction of policy. The future, we have seen, holds immense promise. Tourism can provide the much sought for but elusive push for self-sustained economic growth. The future is also going to be far more competitive than it has been so far. India's ability to achieve growth of tourism comparable to its potentials, will largely depend on the professionalism in the management of the related issues, and its dynamism in response to the emerging trends. As the WTO report sums up - "As tourism enters a new millennium and the prospect of continued expansion and greater importance in the world economy, it faces numerous challenges. Policymakers will increasingly have to address fundamental issues related to the industry's growth, direction and effects"[1]

The Emerging Trends

It is essential for India's tourism planning to integrate with the global trends. The future strategy, therefore, should be largely shaped by the emerging and projected trends in the world, though the compulsions of domestic tourism should continue to be a dominant force guiding our vision and plan of action. **When the tourism attractions enjoyed by both domestic and foreign tourists are the same, and the requirements of infrastructure are broadly similar, the dichotomy between foreign tourists and domestic ones need not be pushed too far. In fact they should merge on a futuristic horizon of tourism planning.**

The WTO has analysed the emerging trends and the factors which will influence the future growth pattern of tourism. Travel and tourism is a social phenomenon deeply influenced by economic factors as also by a complex intermixture of a hoard of others that are likely to shape the future of mankind. It will be worthwhile to have a brief look at some of these future trends.

The growth of tourism so far, as has been pointed out is very impressive. The World Tourism Organization (WTO) has made some projections of future growth on the basis of the observed trends of development so far and on their assessment of the emerging trends and the factors likely to shape the future. These projections throw up vistas of very exciting possibilities in the future and draw attention to interesting issues which will influence the way the possibilities shape up in different countries and regions.

The following table shows the world forecasts region-wise for the year 2020:

Forecasts of International Tourist Arrivals Worldwide and by Region, 1995-2020 (Tourist arrivals-million)

	Base Year	*Forecasts*			*Average Annual Growth Rate (%)*		
Region	*1995*	*2000*	*2010*	*2020*	*1995-2000*	*2000-2010*	*2010-2020*
Africa	20	27	46	75	6.0	5.6	5.1
Americas	111	134	195	285	3.9	3.8	3.8
East Asia/ Pacific	80	116	231	438	7.7	7.2	6.6
Europe	335	390	527	717	3.1	3.1	3.1
Middle East	14	19	37	69	6.9	6.7	6.5
South Asia	4	6	11	19	6.4	6.2	5.8
World	564	692	1,047	1,602	4.2	4.2	4.4

Source: World Tourism Organization (WTO). Tourism 2020 Vision, 1997.

The WTO's projections contained in the 'Vision 2020' also make a comprehensive analysis of some other important emerging trends.

Understanding of these issues that are likely to shape the tourism scenario of the future should be of invaluable help to the policy-planners and the decision-makers of the future. There is no doubt that most of these trends are dependent on many other factors which are not constant and will change with changes in other interdependent variables. Yet, they are very useful indicators of the types of influences that are likely to determine the future growth.

Some of the important observations of WTO are summarised below[2]:

(i) By 2020, there will be 1.6 billion international tourist arrivals and tourism receipts will rise to a staggering US $ 2000 billion.

Forecast of International Tourist Arrivals, 1995-2020

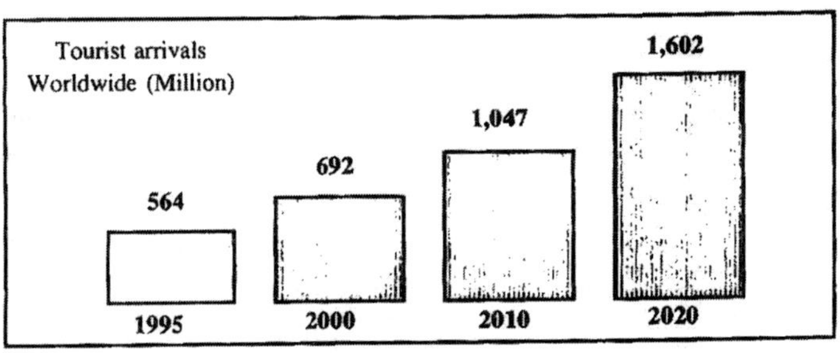

Source : World Tourism Organisation (WTO)

(ii) These figures represent sustained average annual growth rates of 4.3 per cent and 6.7 per cent respectively for arrivals and receipts which is 'far above the maximum probable expansion of 3 per cent per annum in the world's wealth'.

(iii) In spite of such tremendous growth, only 7 per cent of the population of the world will, in fact, be potential tourists. Therefore, 'the industry truly still is in its infancy', and the future potentials are far greater than what has been projected.

(iv) The top ten tourist receiving countries will undergo major changes with China becoming the top destination by 2020.

World's Top Destinations—2020

Country	*Tourist arrivals (Million)*	*Market share (%)*	*Percentage growth rate per annum 1995-2020*
1. China	137.1	8.6	8.0
2. United States	102.4	6.4	3.5
3. France	93.3	5.8	1.8
4. Spain	71.0	4.4	2.4
5. Hong Kong (SAR)	59.3	3.7	7.3
6. Italy	52.9	3.3	2.2
7. United Kingdom	52.8	3.3	3.0
8. Mexico	48.9	3.1	3.6
9. Russian Federation	47.1	2.9	6.7
10. Czech Republic	44.0	2.7	4.0

(v) Similarly, there will be changes in the top ten tourist generating countries. Japan, China and Russian Federation will emerge as major outbound tourism countries.

World's Top Outbound Countries—2020

Country	*Total arrivals generated world wide (Million)*	*Market share (%)*
1. Germany	163.5	10.2
2. Japan	141.5	8.8
3. United States	123.3	7.7
4. China	100.0	6.2
5. United Kingdom	96.1	6.0
6. France	37.6	2.3
7. Netherlands	35.4	2.2
8. Canada	31.3	2.0
9. Russian Federation	30.5	1.9
10. Italy	29.7	1.9
Total (1-10)	788.9	49.2

Source: World Tourism Organization (WTO).

(vi) Europe will remain the largest receiving region though the growth will be below the global average and, therefore, its share in the world market will decline from 59 per cent to 45 per cent.

(vii) East Asia and the Pacific will grow at the rate of 7 per cent per annum and will emerge as the second largest receiving region. Its shares in total arrivals will increase to 27 per cent and thereby it will overtake the Americas.

(viii) South Asia will grow at the rate of 6.1 per cent per annum but its share, in arrivals during the period will grow only from 0.7 percent to 1.2 per cent.

Forecast of International Tourist Arrivals by Region, 1995-2020

Regions	*Tourist arrivals (Million)*			
	1995	*2000*	*2010*	*2020*
Europe	335	390	527	717
East Asia/Pacific	80	116	231	438
Americas	111	134	195	284
Africa	20	27	46	75
Middle East	14	19	37	69
South Asia	4	6	11	19

(ix) There will be a rise in the longhaul share of arrivals and, therefore, increase in inter-regional travel.

Intra-regional/Long-Haul Split of International Tourist Arrivals Worldwide, 1995-2020

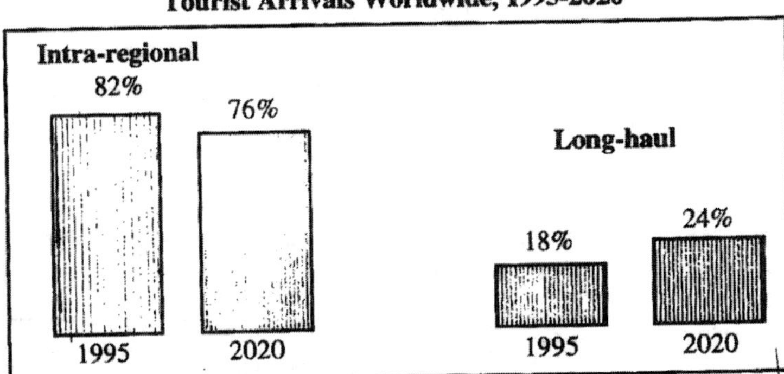

Source: World Tourism Organization (WTO)

Whether these projections turn out to be true as the new century unfolds, will no doubt, depend on the interplay of a large number of complex factors which are sometimes independent of each other and which are not always entirely within the control of the national government or the tourism promotion agencies.

The future growth pattern will be affected largely by increasing competitiveness among nations. To what extent the future tourism growth materializes in a projected manner in any particular country, will depend largely on the conscious determination of the national government to make tourism an engine of growth, and its ability to be one up on its competitors.

It is quite clear that the next century will be dominated by phenomenal growth in travel and tourism. This future growth will also be marked by keener competition and will be influenced by sharply focussed options available to the individuals. It is only logical that any future agenda for action for tourism in India and the broad objectives of development should show sensitivity to such issues.

INDIA : ACTION PLAN

A pragmatic future plan of action should normally be based on two key parameters, viz. -

(i) Assessment of the ground realities.

(ii) Based on such an assessment, making effective plans which, in management terms, will imply -

(a) setting down the objectives;

(b) taking stock of the organisational capabilities to achieve those objectives; and

(c) assessing the physical, financial and human resources available to implement the objectives.

The Constraints

The ground realities of the Indian tourism scenario, oft repeated though they are, can briefly be summarised as follows:-

(1) Inadequacy of infrastructure and poor quality of available infrastructure is one of the most nagging bottlenecks of tourism development. While all areas of infrastructure development need attention, some key elements can be listed as:

(a) carrying capacity by air, roads and railways;

(b) clean and comfortable lodging facilities at reasonable prices;

(c) trained guides and tourist amenities of international standard, in major places of tourist attractions; and

(d) adequate entry points, more international airports, and facilitation services of international norms in the major airports.

(2) While the required infrastructure is inadequate and is not of comparable quality, resources to make qualitative changes quickly and effectively are also not available. Budgetary support to the tourism sector has been insignificant due to pressing and competing demand from various sectors. It is important, therefore, to consider other avenues for resource generation and also to consider modalities for greater public-private partnership.

(3) Tourism is a service industry and the excellence of services makes the crucial difference. That difference comes from trained professional personnel. Shortage of trained manpower, in India, is a serious handicap.

(4) The cost of image building abroad is very high and the negative multiplier effect of adverse publicity as was illustrated in the recent case of a false scare of plague, for example, can be quite damaging. The falling value of the rupee in recent times has made overseas promotion even more expensive and therefore, in real terms, the resources available have been stagnant.

(5) Publicity through brochures and official handouts is only one of the means of reaching out to the people. It is universally recognized that a satisfied tourist is a country's best publicity. Similarly, unhappy experiences of tourists can ruin years of image building exercise. Hassles of travels in India is a major constraint of tourism promotion.

(6) Many of the tourist attractions in India have shown signs of wear and tear because of very high pressure of visitors and poor maintenance. This is another area of very serious concern because with tremendous growth in domestic tourism, the priceless heritage of the country has deteriorated over the years. Public funds for the purpose of maintenance and restoration being limited, their maintenance which is expensive and which requires a high degree of technical expertise, has suffered.

(7) The need to preserve the heritage and natural attractions for posterity is well recognized in government policy. At the same time, as demand for services around such places increases with growth of tourism, the local population sees an opportunity for maximum economic gain out of it within the shortest possible time. This conflict of interest has raised serious issues of sustainable development in many places. Places like Goa and the beaches of Kovalam have shown signs of such stress. At the same time, such issues are now more in the scrutiny of social action groups and media. As a result, in many places tourism promotion has also encountered emerging social tension.

BROAD OBJECTIVES OF FUTURE TOURISM DEVELOPMENT IN INDIA

1 TOURISM AS A NATIONAL AGENDA FOR ACTION

As has been noted above, all the recent Five Year Plans, the National Tourism Policy 1982 and other official documents on tourism development like the National Action Plan (NAP) have focussed on some of the important contributions of tourism as noted below :

(a) Tourism is an important activity for employment generation. Compared to other sectors, employment generation in tourism stands out on a few issues.

- Firstly, the direct and indirect employment is high. Tourism in India contributes of 2.4 per cent of the workforce. Direct employment is estimated to be 9.1 million in 1997, while indirect employment is estimated to be 12.3 million. Considering the inadquacies of our statistical accounting system, the estimation of indirect employment may be quite on the lower side.
- Secondly, multiplier effect of employment generation in tourism is considered to be quite high. The rough official estimate is stated to be 1:1.6.
- Thirdly, according to Government sample surveys, employment generation in tourism, per rupee invested is much higher than agriculture or manufacturing sector. For every million rupees

invested at 1985-86 prices, employment created in some sectors were estimated to be as follows —

Sector	*Jobs*
Agriculture	44.7
Manufacturing	12.6
Mining and quarrying	2.6
Railways	0.9
Other transport	13.8
Tourism	47.5
(Hotel & Resturant)	89.0

Source: Central Statistical Organisation (C.S.O.) Enterprise Survey 1983-84
Ministry of Tourism, Government of India.

- Fourthly, employment in tourism is created wherever tourism attractions exist. Therefore such employment generation is widely dispersed and is generally away from metropolitan cities. The objective of balanced regional development is very well served by tourism.
- Last but not the least, the demand for local handicraft and handloom products gets a boost from tourism development. In India, such activities are to a large extent, a supplementary occupation for the cultivators and women in rural areas. Tourism therefore directly helps in employment and income generation for women and rural artisans.

(b) Tourism is primarily seen as an instrument for earning foreign exchange. The impact may not always be visible, as in budgetary jargon such earnings are grouped as 'invisibles'. But in India it is today the second largest `net' foreign exchange earner in the country.

(c) Many of the Government policy statements have talked about tourism's role in national integration, wider understanding of people and cultures, and in building a spirit of adventure and sport among the youth. These are gains which are not measurable. As such they often go unnoticed. In today's world of unrest and lack of understanding, however imperciptible this role may be, it is becoming increasingly significant.

Many more important dimensions of tourism have been talked about and have been widely recognised. But in India a comprehensive agenda for tourism development as an important and integrated segment of the national planning process, is yet to emerge. Those who are less informed about tourism and look upon tourism only as an elitist pastime, can ask the question, "why tourism?" To answer such a question it would be pertinent to quote the experience of Mexico, which is today one of the top ten destinations of the world. The Mexican experience is beautifully narrated by Mr Antonio Savignac, who apart from being the Secretary General of World Tourism Organisation, was also the Planning and Finance Minister of Mexico.

"This story begins in the mid-'60s. The Bank of Mexico (my country's Central Bank, charged with the issuance of currency and monetary policy) had a problem.

The aim of the Government was to achieve a 6 per cent average annual real rate of growth of the Gross Domestic Product (GDP), while maintaing a low level of inflation. The reason, to absorb an increase of population, then about 3.5 per cent annually, and provide 2.5 percent for growth and social improvement.

The problem: 6 per cent growth meant an increase in *production*; increases in production meant increases in *imports* (goods and services); increasing imports meant obtaining more foreign currency, particularly from the *export* of goods and sevices, to pay for the increased imports.

The question: How to increase exports sufficiently to equilibrate the balance of payments?

The search: An exhaustive on-going analysis was made of all types of goods and services that could be exported: agricultural, fisheries, mining, manufactured and semi-manufactured goods, in-bound (or free port) industries, etc. All types of assumptions, combinations and projections were run through, and several promising leads were further developed, including an export financing scheme for manufactured and semi-manufactured goods, and what eventually became a highly succesful in-bond plant industry.

However, one of the curious activities that continually kept appearing was the case of tourism. Tourism to Mexico had been growing consistently and succesfully in various destinations, particularly on the Pacific Coast (Acapulco, Puerto Vallarta, Mazatlan, etc.) without any planning, fiscal incentives, or credit facilities and despite a whole series of red-tape and lack of facilitation.

A strange beast that seemed to grow like a weed, with no fertilizer, irrigation, care or attention.

Knowing nothing about this activity, we promptly set out to analyze it. This included field trips to Europe, the Mediterranean, the Caribbean, the Pacific and generally, to the more popular sites and destinations.

Our conclusions were surprising at least to us, who were novices in this field.

1. It could be developed and promoted almost anywhere.
2. It grew with little if any government help, programs or policies.
3. It offered an infinity of products and possibilities such as business, conventions, cruises, nature (parks, lakes, mountains), archeology, cities, sports, adventure, sun and beaches, culture, folklore, music, astronomy and so forth.
4. It was relatively free of restrictions, unlike other exports of goods and commodities which were subject to quotas, taxes, import permits and many others.
5. It generally did not consume non-renewable resources, nor did it involve dangerous processes.
6. It was labour intensive and, being a personal service, hard to automate or replace.
7. The technology for its development was well known and easily available, with no major technological changes foreseen or any risk of premature obsolescence.
8. Training of personnel was generally easy, available and quick (except for managerial posts) with minimum requisites of previous studies or training (as opposed to high-tech industries).
9. Foreign tourism was capable of providing an ever increasing flow of foreign currency.
10. The foreign import component of the industry was exceptionally low (excluding airplanes). It was estimated to be of only 6 to 8 percent of the total investments, as compared to 35 to 45 percent for the automobile industry. This meant most of the investments and expenditures would remain in the country, with little foreign currency impact.
11. The expenditures by foreign and national tourists would be spread over a wide variety of business, big and small. For example, excluding air transport, for every 100 units spent in the

country the breakdown was estimated to be :

– Lodging	30—35 per cent
– Food and beverages	20—25 per cent
– Handicrafts	10—15 per cent
– Local transportation	10 per cent
– Shopping, guides, entertainment, etc.	20—25 per cent

12. The tourist expenditure within the country is almost always equivalent to cash (credit cards, traveller cheques, currency). This means immediate cash flow, as compared to the financing of conventional export products.

We were amazed to find this hidden and, to us, unknown jewel but our biggest surprise, what really *made it unique*, was the *way* the product is consumed.

How so? Well, traditionally products, be they industrial (machinery, equipment, etc.) or agricultural (cereals, vegetables, fruits, etc.), consumer goods (electronic, clothes, medicines, cars, toys, etc.), or others, regardless of where they are produced, (Japan, Germany, Korea, the USA, or in major cities) must be shipped and delivered for their use or consumption where the purchaser or client resides.

This means packing, transporting, distributing and servicing the product, including inventories, 'losses, delays, insurance and financing among many others.

Tourism, in this respect, is unique because the consumer must displace himself along with his money, to his destination, be it for a convention, business meeting, sightseeing, or any of the myriad tourism products.

This makes tourism an *incredibely agile and flexible* tool for economic and social development. Why? Let's look at other more traditional activities: *agriculture* can be developed and is limited in its scope to the availability of *sun, water and climate* among others. Mining can only be developed where the resource is found. Industry tends to concentrate in or near the large centers of consumption, where it finds the needed infrastructure, energy, personnel, technicians, suppliers, etc.

Tourism, on the other hand, given its enormous variety of segments, for all tastes and budgets, can truly be developed almost anywhere there is something of interest to do or enjoy.

To make a longer story slightly shorter, the Mexican Government concluded that if tourism had grown so well and so consistently, with little, if any, encouragement what would it not do with some help and support in planning, financing, promotion, facilitation and political and budgetary backing"[3]

2 WHAT SHOULD BE THE TARGET OF TOURIST ARRIVALS-FOREIGN AND DOMESTIC

The fundamental question has been raised often and needs to be debated more. In the Indian context, while discussing the question, certain parameters which influence the boundaries of our action must be taken into account. One is the known pressure of a large size of population, and consequential problems caused by increasing numbers every year. Tourism infrastructure like the roads, railways, civic amenities, etc., are the same as are used by the general masses. The available infrastructure has to first take care of the basic needs of the growing numbers. Existing capacity of the country to absorb a large number of tourists being limited by inadequate infrastructure. There is, a view that we should plan not in terms of numbers of foreign tourists, but of earnings. The answer to this debate depends on a variety of factors, most important being the physical capacity to attract any particular number. The projections in the official documents about the future growth of tourist arrivals are not very clear and except for the National Action Plan, other documents have not mentioned any figure. The National Action Plan, 1992 aimed at attracting 1per cent of the international tourist arrivals in the world within five years, which in effect means that by 1997, the country should have about 6 million arrivals . The actuals, as is known, is only 2.37 million. Happily the growth in earnings has been steady, but for both counts the mismatch between the projection and achievements continue. Pragmatism would dictate that preoccupation with numbers and targets be diluted, but then one has to accept the fact that any plan of action without a quantified target becomes too general.

In 1996, tourist arrivals increased by 8 per cent. If this growth rate can be maintained the realistic estimate of international arrivals would be about 3.37 million by 2001. But, again a growth rate of 8 per cent depends on a large number of imponderables. Already in 1997, the rate of growth declined to 5 per cent. The 9th Plan Working Group Report of the Planning Commission of India was on the other hand, more optimistic in estimating

5.95 million arrivals by 2001. Similarly, foreign exchange earning was projected as US $ 8.1 billion by 2001. Both these projections were based on the strategy and targets outlined in the National Action Plan 1992.

The arrival projections depend largely on the scale and pace of investment for creation of adequate tourism infrastructure. In another official exercise done through a 'Strategy Paper', the quantum of investment required to achieve a target of 5 million arrivals by 2000 AD was estimated to be Rs. 45000 crore. The estimates are as follows :

Rs. (Crores)

Investment in	*Central Government*	*State Government*	*Financial Institutions*	*Private*	*Total*
• Infrastructure					
• Airports					
• Air seat capacity					
• Railways					
• Roads				4350	
Total	20150	4100	1000	29600	
• Tourism product development	4861	500	9000	4600	18461
Grand total	25,011	4600	10000	8950	48561

Such a level of investment has not been possible so far and going by the present trends, does not appear feasible in the near future. Moreover, all such investments have a time-lag. Therefore, in the short-run, the alternative strategy of thinking more in terms of earnings rather than arrivals, should merit more attention. Tourism planning in future must concentrate on what has been talked about always but not yet achieved — selective segmented development of product and infrastructure, targeted marketing and excellence in service.

The number of domestic tourists was estimated to be around 150 million in 1996. This estimate did not include the religious tourists who do not utilise conventional paid accommodation. This number is expected to grow substantially in the coming years because with the projected Gross Domestic Product (GDP) growth of 7 per cent and above, the general condition of the people will improve and a larger number of people will have the means and leisure to travel. The number of domestic tourists is an important element of all Indian tourism planning. The scale, however, is totally out of proportion with the observed global trends. Whereas the average world ratio of domestic to foreign tourist is 10:1 approximately, in India it is a staggering proportion of 65:1. The inescapable reality of India's future tourism planning is, therefore, that such planning must be built around the demand of the local markets and of domestic tourists.

3 ECO-FRIENDLY SUSTAINABLE DEVELOPMENT

The importance of a dynamic policy of sustainable tourism development has been explained in Chapter 5. Such a policy must be the corner-stone of any future vision. The gifts of nature and endowments of history and civilisation are non-renewable. The future policy, therefore, must be to enhance the quality of the inheritance and to leave to the future generations a better and richer heritage. Such an objective can be achieved only by a mixture of various measures like, pragmatic regulations, their effective enforcement, extensive public awareness programmes and constructive and continuous mechanism for public participation.

4 IMPORTANCE OF CREATING AWARENESS AND PEOPLE'S PARTICIPATION

Tourism is a multisectoral activity. However good may be the intentions behind government policy, however comprehensive the planning may be, they will be ineffective unless they are woven into the understanding of all the sectors involved. Creating awareness about the importance of tourism, and about the need for sustainable tourism, therefore, is an important element of tourism action plan. Such awareness compaigns may have several elements. Firstly, there should be awareness about the socio-economic importance of tourism. The common perception about tourism as an elitist activity should change and people must realise tourism's multifaceted role. Secondly, such awareness compaigns should lead to the growth of a movement for public action in various areas of sustainable tourism development. One can reasonably expect that once such a movement for public action is generated by the awareness compaign, it will also lead to the emergence of a culture of tourism. India has a tradition of hospitality but not yet an atmosphere of spontaneous friendliness to tourists. That message of Pandit Nehru : 'Welcome a tourist and send back a friend', should be the byword of tourism campaign in India in the new century.

Naturally, such awareness can be meaningful if it percolates down to all the different segments of the government who contribute to making the total tourism service, - the policy makers, the legislators, the bureaucrats and the common people who come in touch with the tourists in various ways. Without such a comprehensive awareness, tourism will continue to be a segmented departmental activity, and not a culture for the people.

Similarly, such awareness and emergence of a tourism-friendly culture, in tune with our old philosophy of **"Vasudhaiva Kutumbakam"** can be possible only if the people actively participate and share the vision of the government about the multi-dimensional role of tourism. Such involvement of the people should be comprehensive but more prominently should be in some of the following specific areas :

(a) People should participate in preserving the cultural heritage and in preventing any tendency to vulgarise such heritage through unwise commercial exploitation.

(b) People should also take pride in the rich endowments of history and nature around them and should get involved in maintaining the quality of such products. Preservation of our heritage can become a national commitment only when the people take pride in them.

(c) Common people will participate in such activities only when they perceive benefits flowing from such participation. People must share the benefits that development of tourism brings locally. Such economic sharing will strengthen the nature of participation and will also strengthen their resolve to take care of the tourism attractions that provide them such income.

What should be the mechanism for ensuring such participation? Making participation very formalised will rob it of the very essence of participation. In fact if the methods of participation are formalised, the basic purpose may be lost in burcaucratic hassles. India has achieved tremendous progress in democratic decentralisation with decision-making powers flowing to the people at the grassroot levels. It is at this level that the tourism planning could be integrated to the district plans. At present, tourism plans are seen primarily as the responsibility of the Ministry of Tourism and, therefore, tourism remains outside the active interest of the people who can get benefit out of it. Some States have derived good results of public participation by involving the local community in the decision-making process through 'advisory councils'. There is understandable scepticism about interminable committees making tourism promotion even more complicated. Yet, it is undeniable that such councils can provide an opening for honest, sincere and good intentioned people to contribute to tourism.

5 IMPROVING THE QUALITY OF SERVICES

Tourism, we have noted, is a service industry and the quality of service makes all the difference between competing destinations. We have seen that in India there is a tremendous shortage of trained manpower in the hospitality sector at present. On a rough estimate of about 30,000 hotel rooms that are in the pipeline and 30,000 more that are required immediately, the total manpower requirement to service the hospitality sector has been projected to be about 20,000 per year. Against such a requirement, the actual output from the Government institutions is only about 5,000 per year. Even if all the other private institutions are taken into account, the total availability of trained manpower does not exceed 10,000 in a year. More private initiative in this area therefore, is necessary. If India is to achieve higher targets of tourist arrivals, more hotels, more restaurants and wayside amenities will have to be created within a very short time. The requirement of trained manpower will also, therefore, increase substantially. A comprehensive human resource development programme should, therefore, be a key element of future policy. Such a programme of human resource development should also cover orientation of the staff at airports, customs facilitation, guides, etc., on a continuous basis.

6 NEED FOR A NEW THRUST IN IMAGE-BUILDING

As pointed out in the WTO study referred to earlier, in future, consumers will have an increasing say in the choice of destinations. Destinations will be under closer scrutiny of the consumers. Tourists' choice will be guided by various factors that create an image about a country. Issues of environment and ecological preservation, human rights violations, child sex abuses, etc., will be important factors in such decision process. The focus of the media has already been quite sharp on such issues and this interest in likely to grow in future. The Central and State Governments will, therefore, not only have to be sensitive to such global issues, such sensitivity must be reflected in the visible action of the government.

With greater access to information technology, and greater awareness about specific issues of global concern, the choice of destinations in future in expected to be a more weighed option than it has been hitherto. How a tourist will decide between competing destinations will be influenced greatly by the image that is formed in his mind about a particular country. The image–building exercise of India will therefore need qualitative change and professional management.

While revolution in information technology will make access to information easy, advances in transport technology will open up immense possibilities for larger, faster, better aircraft and better mode of internal communication. Tourists will have wider choice and other things being equal, will prefer destinations with better communication facilities. Places without such facilities will be edged out in the keen competition even if they have good tourist attractions.

Singapore, for example, has capitalised on its reputation for excellent facilities and services to attract larger number of tourists than India which has a distinct edge over Singapore in respect of tourist products.

Such an image–building exercise will be facilitated by rigorous implementation of air safety standards. Perception of safety vary. Tourists generally look for fun and relaxation. Spread of international terrorism and terrorist activities which target tourists may affect some regions, as it has, for example affected Egypt. Similarly, international air travel is likely to be marked by great improvements in technology in operation. Such improvements are expected to make travels cheaper, easier and safer. Naturally, the great tourism boom will be vitally linked to progress in air transport technology. Whatever it is, one thing seems certain, that the air corridors will be far more crowded than it is today. A country's reputation about air safety standard will undoubtedly influence tourists' decision on destination choice.

The search for safety and security is likely to extend beyond air travels. Health and hygiene will also be high on the scrutiny of tourists. Already, most countries have tightened up regulations for controlling the spread of AIDS. The tourists' perception about the danger of serious infectious diseases will be a factor in the overall options for the choice of destinations.

The implications of such developments can be sumed up as follows —

(a) The marketing strategy should be designed to address these concerns of the tourists. Therefore, marketing will have to be more aggressive and more focussed. WTO studies have projected that there will be an increase in the long-haul traffic and thus more inter-regional arrivals. The developing trends in household economic growth, individual work norms, etc., implies that people will tend to favour more than one short holiday a year rather than a long yearly holiday. Such behavioural patterns will need close scrutiny and marketing strategy should be flexible enough to adjust to such changing requirements. At the same time, the pattern and sources of inbound and outbound tourists are not static phenomena. Influenced by a variety of socio-economic factors, they keep changing. It will be necessary to look closely at the emerging sources of outbound tourists and to focus more attention to marketing in those areas. China and the Russian Federation, for example, will emerge as important sources of outbound tourists with 71 million and 47 million people respectively from these countries travelling abroad by 2020. Japan will continue to be an important outbound source. Our marketing strategy should become tailor-made dictated by our options and new opportunities and should not be tied down to traditional markets and traditional strategies.

(b) It follows, therefore, that to tap the outbound tourists from different segments, the marketing strategy should be varied and suited to the particular consumer tastes. For example, recent studies have shown that most Japanese tourists are in the age group of 45 and above. They are generally economically well-off and travel primarily for relaxation and spiritual satisfaction. They are extremely safety conscious and particular about the quality and reliability of services. Any marketing plan which targets such tourists must take into account such micro details of tourists. In a sense, marketing will have to be not only professional but also a very seriously studied series of flexible strategies.

(c) As most tourists, both individually and in groups will have access to latest facilities of information technology and will be making use of these to access information, our technology in marketing should be compatible with the world-system.

7 IMPROVING ORGANISATIONAL CAPABILITIES

The agenda for action for the future is crowded. Time, however, is of essence and there is an element of urgency in trying to do what is, in any analysis, an essential agenda if India really plans to fully exploit its tourism potentials. Even if the private sector plays an important and increasing role in the future scenario, as we have noted, the role of the Government will continue to be of the prime-mover. The role of the Ministry of Tourism in the Central Government, as well as in the States will be of a catalyst and of a coordinator. With manifold increase in the expanse of the activities, this role will be more complicated and sensitive.

In the Indian scenario, there is some amount of haziness, and some ambiguity about the respectives roles of the Central Government and of the State Governments. Tourism is not just one subject but a conglomeration of many sectoral activities. This may be one reason for which tourism as such does not find any place in either the *Central List* or the *State List* or the *Concurrent List* in the Schedule of the Constitution of India. By convention, the States have played the primary role in the development of tourism. Most of the activities like development of tourism infrastructure, protection of environment, regulatory powers for law and order, sanitation, hygiene, land development, etc., are within the control of the State Government. Yet, if the tourism activities expand the way projected, requiring diverse activities to be dovetailed, the question of overriding jurisdiction may arise. There may be a need for Central Legislation to enforce uniformity or to remove hindering imbalances between regions. The necessity of clearly defining the respective roles of the Central Government and of the State Governments or of providing a legal basis for coordinated and harmonious action by both, should be a step towards building a strong organisational structure.

Moreover, as India tries to catch up for lost time and strives to achieve a vast expanse of activities managed by different agencies within a short period, coordination will become more desirable and more difficult than ever before. Even at the macro level, there are too many agencies directly involved. 'First, the Central, State and the Union Territories' governments play the most crucial role. Second, in each of them, it is not one Department that is fully responsible for all the activities, but many Departments, each jointly and severally responsible for the ultimate tourism product. For example, at the Central Government level, the activities of the following Departments vitally affect the overall tourism promotion—

(a) Department of Culture (Archaeological Survey of India — for regulation, preservation and maintenance of the cultural and historical heritage).

(b) Civil Aviation — (For air seats, airport controls and air safety).

(c) Raiways and Surface Transport (For internal communication).

(d) Customs and Excise (Airport facilitation).

(e) Home Department (Safety of tourists, immigration facilitation).

(f) Environment (Regulation of environmental norms).

(g) Urban Development (Civic amenities, sanitation and hygiene. land and building regulations for hotels, lodges, etc.).

(h) Finance, Industry and Commerce — (incentives to the private sector).

(i) External Affairs (Visa, external publicity).

The list in only illustrative and not exhaustive. We have seen earlier that about 30 different activities are linked to the development of tourism and all these, in their impact will cover all aspects of government activities. For instance, the Department of Handicrafts and Handlooms or Small Scale Industries depend heavily on tourism and tourism growth may involve appropriate development of these activities as well.

Even the private sector is not a homogenous identity. We have seen that WTTC has identified upwards of 30 activities which are directly or indirectly linked to tourism. Among them, however, the tour operators, the travel agents, transporters and the hoteliers are the more prominent players. These sectors often represent different interest groups and such interests are sometimes in conflict with each other. It is desirable, but difficult to forge a common platform of different disparate elements making crucial contributions to promotion of tourism. Yet, some sort of arrangement to achieve a common approach is very desirable. Different countries have tried different methods to achieve such coordination within the government agencies, between government agencies and the private sector and again within the different elements of the private sector itself. Of relevance in this context is the organizational framework worked out in USA under the initiative of the President of USA. The broad framework is reproduced below:

National Tourism Strategy
Structural framework

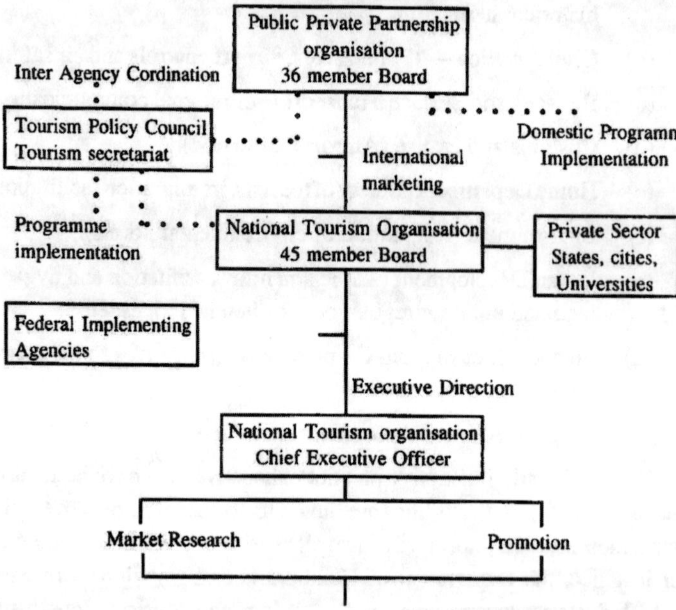

Organisational Structure

Administrative organisation is important to achieve the policy goals. Strengthening of the administrative arrangements in India must go hand in hand with wider spectrum that government policies try to encompass.

The need for an efficient organisation to help in achieving the objectives has been discussed for a long time. Mr Chib in his book has traced the history of academic discussion on a proper organisation for tourism. As far back as 1968-69, the Indian Institute of Public Administration was asked to advise on the matter. In 1971, the UNDP group of experts led by Dr Timoty O'Discall reviewed the Indian tourism secenario and submitted its report. The UNDP Report basically favoured a change-over from the Government department to a non-statutory commission as a National Tourism Authority. The Committee submitted a number of arguments in support of this change-over in organisational pattern. The National Committee on Tourism in its report in 1988 has categorically recommended setting up of a National Tourism Board. It recommends as follows :

"Recognising the growing potential of tourism for earning foreign exchange, generating employment, preserving cultural heritage, helping in national integration and assisting in development of backward areas, it is necessary to provide for a structure which would not suffer from problems of overlap and inadequate tourism management skill. It is,. therefore, recommended that an apex body called the National Tourism Board should be set-up."[4]

A possible organizational structure for India's tourism organisation could be as follows :

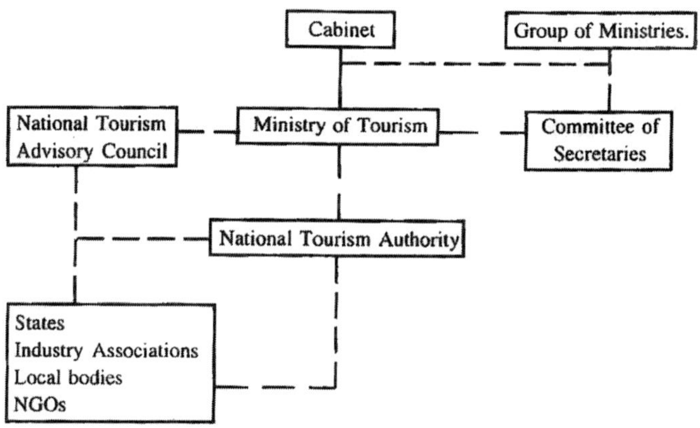

In the ultimate analysis, the efficacy of any policy lies in its implementation. Many of the objectives outlined above can be achieved only in the long-run. However, looking through the history of development of tourism in India one is amazed to find that what has been talked about here as a future vision has been talked about long back almost in identical language. Mr S.N. Chib who was the first Director General of Tourism in India, in his Sardar Patel Memorial Lecture in 1981, had this to say–

"Thirty years ago when I started on the great adventure of promoting tourism I had hopes that we would become one of the leaders of this movement. We were endowed with unique tourist resources and we had talent. It seemed that the sky was the limit. I believed in the Aristotelian doctrine that knowledge is a condition of what is best, and if we were able to establish that tourism would benefit us and improve the quality of life, a purposeful policy would follow."[5] Mr. Chib goes on to outline the plan of action for future, which, if we are not aware that they were made in 1981, will sound extremely topical today.

If these observations appear to be too familiar today, then one has to realise that the answer to our maladies is not in a proliferation of policies and objectives but in getting down to the brasstacks and in taking action on small issues which are entirely within the control of those who are involved in promotion of tourism.

8 LOOKING FOR OTHER AREAS OF RESOURCE GENERATION

The main hurdle that everyone would point out–both government and the private sector - is the lack of resources. In a country like India with ever increasing population, where the government have very pressing priorities of sorting out the problems of basic human needs, resources available for other activities are bound to be less than required. One has, therefore, to look at other alternatives and to pursue them rationally. Some of the ways in which the available resources can be augmented are –

(i) Overseas assistance for promotion of tourism infrastructure can be one area of augmenting government resources for basic infrastructure. Experience of some such overseas financing like the OECF financing in Ajanta and Ellora and in the Buddhist Circuit of Bihar and Uttar Pradesh has shown that imaginative projects taken up can have far-reaching implications for growth of other infrastructure as well. Tourism does not find a high priority in the portfolio of projects prioritised for external assistance. This situation needs to be selectively modified.

(ii) In China, reportedly about 20 billion dollars of direct foreign investment flows into the tourism sector every year. In India tourism has been accepted as a priority sector for foreign direct investment, where upto 100 per cent foreign equity participation is possible. Yet, the direct foreign investment flows have been very negligible. There are many reasons for such unsatisfactory flows, many of which would be similar to those applicable to other sectors as well. Delays in approvals, multiplicity of agencies and complexity of approval procedure, lack of suitable incentives, etc., are cited as general constraints. It is essential to have a very close look at this area and to pursue a pragmatic policy designed to ensure that the liberalisation process shows results in action.

(iii) Tourism is contributing substantially to employment and income generation and the sector is providing substantial resources to all the State Governments in the form of revenues from various taxes, apart from huge foreign exchange earnings, It is only appropriate that some portion of the earnings. Is ploughed back to the sector so that it generates much larger income to the country as a whole. In a sense, the possibility of creating a pool account out of the tourism earnings like that of the Oil Pool Account could be considered. Such a move will be cost-effective, as such funds judiciously used will ensure larger income and revenue generation.

(iv) Economic liberalisation has now been on for a few years and the role of the private sector has been duly recognised. Tourism, the policy documents point out, is primarily private sector driven. Yet, institutional mechanism to create that enabling atmosphere where the sector can play its expected role, does not function at the optimal level. Tourism development in the country can be possible only if the resource requirement of a large segment of the sector is taken care of by the private sector. For this to happen, the private sector has to be motivated by incentives envisaged by a transparent policy of partnership and evolved by careful nurturing. At the same time, the private sector must also come out with responsive participation, dispelling the doubts and insinuation that even though the liberalisation process has thrown the cage open, the 'tiger' refuses to come out.

(v) Even within the existing constraints of resources in the public sector, more effective availability of fund for tourism related developments can be found if tourism development planning is integrated with the planning process of the States right from the Panchayat level. In the present scenario, quite a lot of fund for rural development is available at the district level planning. In many of the areas of the country, rural development and employment creation as well as development of craft could be motivated by taking up development of tourism products around that area. Such tourism products need not necessarily be the ones where foreign tourists flock to. The ever-increasing number of domestic tourists in India, composed primarily of a growing middle-class, whose purchasing power and leisure time,will increase with the growth in GDP, can provide the real substance to tourism development. The product development should, therefore, start with the numerous attractions dotting our countryside, which the local community can look after and benefit from their development. It will indeed be a multi-pronged development strategy.

9 MAKING TRAVELS A PLEASURE

Apart from resources, there are many small things which go a l... way in developing a truly tourist friendly culture which can be taken up by the local authorities and the State Governments. One of the most important objectives, and also an urgent one should be to take steps to make travel a pleasant experience for the tourists. Every State can, within the existing structures, ensure that touts and others who cling to any tourist in most places do not hassle them on arrivals or in market places or when they want to enjoy in a relaxed way. This can be done simply by a stricter enforcement of the rules in the areas where tourists come in numbers. Some States have introduced the concept of 'Tourist Police' or 'Tourist Assistance Force'. Imaginative organisation of such types can go a long way in reassuring the tourists and also in spreading the correct message to the people.

10 BASIC CLEAN FACILITIES

One can understand that big infrastructure takes time and money to develop, but it should be possible to provide in the tourist places the basic minimum facilities like clean toilet, drinking water, a place of shelter from sun and rain, if required, and a decent place to buy souvenir items without having to worry about the quality or about the price.

11 GREAT HERITAGE IN A SHABBY SURROUNDING?

Most tourists to India, even those who otherwise feel ecstatic about the great country, would politely talk about the necessity of a cleaner ambience around the grand heritage products that we have. While most of our tourism products, unique in their own way, attract tourists in spite of the surroundings, it is possible that in course of time, such surroundings may be a deterrent factor. Even if comprehensive urban planning arrangements, required as they are, cannot be taken up immediately, yet appropriate maintenance and good upkeep of the minimum vicinity of the tourism products, can go a long way in conveying the sensitivity of the nation to its heritage and in encouraging the tourists to enjoy them. Public-private partnership being the essence of future planning of tourism, private sector's professionalism can perhaps be utilised for this purpose.

12 CLEARER SIGNS

India also has to match other countries in professionalism in the tourism sector. Super highways and public amenities on such highways may come up in due course. But even before that, the roads leading to the tourist places can be spruced up. Local communicities and the private sector, who benefit from such tourist flows, can be made to take pride in maintaining them. Clear international signages can be put up to guide the tourists to places of tourist interest and clear inscriptions explaining the tourism products could be put up to help the tourist understand and enjoy the significance of such attractions.

13 BUILDING A COMMON PLATFORM

The 1982 Policy talked about a common endeavour. It has proved to be an elusive concept. Much more needs to be done to facilitate the private sector, to make land available at reasonable costs, to rationalise the taxation structure so that initiative is not sapped and that India does not become an expensive destination, to streamline investment procedure so that the much talked about 38 approvals required to start an investment becomes only a myth.

14 WHAT TO BUY AND WHERE

In the Indian context, with never-ending markets and infinite variety of products, this question sounds irrelevant but any tourist will say that this is the question uppermost in his mind. There are numerous complaints of harassment by touts, cheating in price and quality and hassles in purchases. Tourists, however budget limited they are, love to take back some memories from the places visited. The entire country cannot boast of a single modern shopping complex offering variety in shopping in one area where the quality and the prices need not cause concern. There is need to properly market quality momentos, books, souvenirs, etc.

The list can go on. To summarise, here are some commonsense suggestions for an action plan for the millennium yatra—

(A) PREPARING FOR THE JOURNEY

(1) The First Contact

— Adequate information to be available on website - information on where to go, how to go, where to stay, etc.

— Modernize Government of India Tourist Offices. Response to tourist's enquiries to be prompt and accurate. Only trained professional staff to man these offices.

— Along with visa, a welcome packet with basic tourist information materials may be given to each person. They may also be given a self-addressed mailer with address printed which they can use to send their comments, suggestions, etc., after the visit.

— Visa procedure to be simplified and computerised. If bilateral reciprocal arrangements can be entered into with major sources of outbound tourists, the ideal situation would be to remove visa requirements with those countries. Alternatively, tourists and short stay visitors may be given visa on arrival.

(2) Ease of access

— Present system of charter flights is very restrictive — being available only in few places. Some places like Goa have restriction of flights to specific hours and days. In the present fiercely competitive atmosphere, such restrictions adversely affect tourist flows. There should be free flow of charters and more stations be opened for charter flights. This will also reduce pressure on the metropolitan cities.

— China has followed a strategy of increasing the number of international airports with great success. We should increase the number of international airports.

— Communication to many potential tourist attractions like Ladakh Andaman & Nicobar (A&N) Island, Lakshadweep Island are inadequate. Flights are inadequate and often, as in Ladakh, the schedules are not announced early. As a result, foreign travel agents can't offer bookings and we lose tourists. These deficiencies have to be removed.

(3) Arrival : The first impression

— All our arrival lounges need special sprucing up, and need to be brought to international standards.

— The scene outside the arrival arena in most airports is one of utter confusion. Touts hassle tourists. This should be sternly regulated - special tourist assistance squad and booths may be provided in each airport.

— Authorised Hotel Associations may be allowed to put up a counter so that hotel booking can be made at the airport. Hotels may be persuaded to provide courtesy coaches or transport on reasonable payment.

— Pre-paid taxi concept should be expanded. Taxis form airport must be of standard design and good quality, to be separately registered. A place can be marked where taxis in serial order will come and pick up whoever is in position in a quece without hassle and harassment.

(B) BEAUTIFICATION AND PRESERVATION OF CRUMBLING HERITAGE

— We have thousands of invaluable heritage sites. Most of them are in poor shape of maintenance. Upkeep outside is equally poor - even the prestigious Red Fort and Taj Mahal precincts leave much to be desired.

— Phased programme of improvement of important places must be taken up. May explore, UNESCO, and other organisations working in this area for augmenting resources. Also local industries can be involved in maintaining the surroundings, as well as in restoration and preservation of important tourist attractions and monuments. One tourist attraction in each State may be taken up every year for such beautification as a common endeavour of all the agencies concerned.

— In such programmes, there should be a plan for improving public convenience and other facilities which are poor in may tourist places. Phased programme of providing world class facilities in each important place should be drawn up. Maintenance of such facilities can be given to private parties like Sulabh International.

— Each nationally important tourist place should have an exclusive 'souvenir shop' at the exit point. Products should be especially manufactured and designed to make these shops exclusive. Beautifully produced tourist information books which can serve as souvenirs to take away, replica of important monuments etc., picture post-cards, handicraft items, small momentos can be sold through such outlets. Special attention should be given to packaging of international standard. Archaeological Survey of India/India Tourism Development Corperation (ASI/ITDC) can jointly float a chain of such shops and a brand image may be built up.

— In important places of tourist attractions, monuments, historical sites, audio guides may be introduced on a commercial basis.

(C) MAKING TRAVELS RELAXING

— A standard design for wayside public amentities should be drawn up. Space should be reserved in all important highways connecting tourist places, say at an interval of every 100 km for such amenities. These may be offered to the private sector for development and construction. Hygiene and maintenace, etc., of these places may be strictly regulated by local authorities or State Tourism Development Corporation. Wherever any filling station is allowed in any National Highway (NH), provision for such amentities may be made compulsory. A programme of putting up 100 such amenities every year may be drawn up.

— All roads/NH leading to important tourist centres must have prominent international signages indicating distance, direction, etc. Phased programme to complete this work within a period of five years may be taken up.

(D) INFRASTRUCTURE WITHIN THE COUNTRY

— Each State must prepare a Master Plan for the development of budget accomodation and earmark land at reasonable cost in the identified areas and desired locations. This action should be taken up as priority, to be completed within 2/3 years.

— Each metropolitan city must develop a modern shopping complex of international standard - a place where tourists can get all the variety of India, a place where they can relax and shop - where they need not worry about the quality or the price. The authority responsible for building it must also ensure strict standards of cleanliness, aesthetics, etc.

— At least one international standard convention centre should be established in each metropolis. Incentive by way of land at reasonable price and other infrastructure needs to be provided and international investment invited to establish such centres commercially.

The list is only suggestive and by no means exhaustive. We have to get to the mindset of thinking that we can do it. One can do it if one looks for simple solutions. In India we need to get away from the oft repeated lip service of pride in our great civilization and culture—an insensitivity that is eroding the past itself. One is reminded of the Sherlock Homes joke which puts the message across beautifully -

> Sherlock Holmes and Doctor Watson were hiking. They hiked all day long and then, tired, went to sleep in the tent. Holmes woke up deep at night, wakes Watson and says, "Watson, do you see the bright stars and do you notice how clear the sky is? What can you deduce from it?"
>
> "Well, this clearly tells us the weather tomorrow is going to be dry and sunny."
>
> "No Watson, it's simpler: The fact that we can see the stars just means that somebody has stolen our tent."

Such small things can make all the difference. One is reminded of Virgil -

"They can
Because
They think, they can."

References

1. WTO : International Tourism : A Global perspective *op cit.*, 1997, p.363.
2. WTO : Tourism 2020 Vision, Executive Summary, 1997, pp. 3-9.
3. Mr Antonio Savignac. "The importance of tourism as an instrument for economic and social development" Foundation Day Lecture, 25 January 1998, New Delhi. (unpublished).
4. Report of the National Committee on Tourism, Planning Commission, Government of India, May 1988, p. 99.
5. S.N. Chib. Essays on Tourism, 1989, p. 45.

APPENDICES

APPENDIX-I

Tourism Policy

1982

Tourism Policy

(Presented by the Minister for Tourism in the Lok Sabha and Rajya Sabha on November 3, 1982)

Dimensions of Tourism

1. Tourism has become a global phenomenon in the Past 30 years. Better and faster means of communications have resulted in a massive movement of people throughout the world drawing them closer through experiencing and appreciating one another's culture and lifestyle. To give an idea of the dimensions of world travel, in 1981 there were about 290 million world travellers who spent US $ 106 billion (Rs. 84,800 crores). In India alone about 5 million people, excluding city commuters, are carried daily by the Railways over their vast networks indicating the strength of domestic travel movement within the country.

Parameters of Tourism

2. The parameters of tourism are wide and far-reaching. From a small beginning of individuals travelling alone in search of adventure, knowledge, trade and pilgrimage, the mass movement of people today all over the world has given rise to a highly sophisticated, multi-disciplinary industry —Tourism — to develop and promote tourist activities, to service the tourist facilities so as to ensure visitor — satisfaction and thus generate more travel. Because tourism promotes exchange of ideas and views and facilitates interaction of people and their culture, it can be a potent instrument for achieving national integration, better international understanding and ultimately peaceful co-existence for the people of the world.

3.1 Despite its world-wide operations, tourism can function in the smallest of settings as effectively and efficiently as in wide-ranging, multinational operations. It has thus the flexibility of adjustments to situations which few industries possess. Tourism can thus be an individual endeavour or it can employ thousands in a single operation. It can be a small enterprise or a multi-million project. Tourism is thus both labour-intensive and capital-intensive activity. In economic terms, tourism is a major source of foreign exchange earnings for many countries. It can help correct adverse trade balances and regional imbalances, create employment opportunities and give a direct stimulus to the socio-economic development of backward areas in a country.

3.2 However, there are pitfalls as well. Unregulated tourism can cause many problems like unbalanced social change and economic development, social tensions and environmental pollution, distortion of lifestyles and cultural decay — indeed the destruction of the very entity on which tourism is built.

Stages of Tourism Development

4.1 Tourism development in India has passed through many stages. At Government level, the development of tourist facilities was taken up in a planned manner from 1956 coinciding with the Second Five Year Plan. The developmental approach has evolved from isolated planning of single unit facilities in the Second and Third Five Year Plans to integrated development in the Fourth Plan (Gulmarg and Kovalam projects), and thereon to integrated area development in the Fifth and Sixth Plans.

4.2 The many attractions and facets of India hold virtually an unlimited potential for tourism development. The endeavour therefore will be to convert this vast potential into reality through well-planned, well-defined and fully integrated national programmes of tourism development.

4.3 The performance in the field of tourism over the past 30 years has been quite impressive. In 1951, 25 million world travellers crossed national frontiers to visit other countries as tourists. Of these, India received 16,829 or only 0.066 per cent. In 1981 while the world tourist movement was estimated at 290 million, India received 8.53 lakh and 4.27 lakh arrivals from Pakistan and Bangladesh or 0.44 per cent. The estimated foreign exchange earnings of India from tourism in 1951 were Rs. 7.7

crores. In 1981 these were estimated at Rs. 702 crores. Hardly any other sector of the economy has recorded such a consistently notable performance.

4.4 In 1951 there were only a few hotels primarily in the metropolitan cities and at hill stations which could cater to the needs of the tourists. There were only a handful of travel agencies. Today there are 371 Government of India approved hotels with 23,620 rooms and 185 approved travel agencies throughout the country.

Objectives

5. The Government's objectives thus are to so develop tourism that :—

(i) It becomes a unifying force nationally and internationally fostering better understanding through travel.

(ii) It helps to preserve, retain and enrich our world-view and lifestyle, our cultural expressions and heritage in all its manifestations. The prosperity that tourism brings must cause accretion and strength rather than damage to our social and cultural values and depletion of our natural resources. In tourism, India must present itself on its own terms — not as an echo or imitation of other countries, other cultures and other lifestyles.

(iii) It brings socio-economic benefits to the community and the State in terms of employment opportunities, income generation, revenue generation for the states, foreign exchange earnings and, in general, causes human-habitat improvement.

(iv) It gives a direction and opportunity to the youth of the country both through international and domestic tourism to understand the aspirations and viewpoints of others and thus to bring about a greater national integration and cohesion.

(v) It also offers opportunities to the youth of the country not only for employment but also for taking up activities of nation-building character like sports, adventure and the like. Thus as a programme for the moulding of the youth of the country, tourism is of inestimable value.

Domestic Tourism

6.1. Domestic tourists travelling within their country form the bulk of world tourist traffic. While domestic tourist statistics are not available at present on an all-India basis, the volume of passenger traffic carried by our

Railways and the road transportation system is indicative of the enormous size of domestic tourism in India. For the large number of our people who travel on pilgrimage or as tourists, facilities provided are minimal. It will, therefore, be our endeavour to substantially improve and expand facilities for domestic tourists.

International Tourism

6.2. Recognising the importance of international tourism in earning foreign exchange and thereby making a major contribution to the national economy as well as in creating international goodwill and understanding, high priority will be accorded to the development of international tourism.

Cultural Tourism

6.3.1 Various surveys and studies have confirmed that the biggest element in attracting international tourists to India is our historical and archaeological monuments. Although the maintenance and upkeep of the monuments is the responsibility of the Archaeological Survey of India and the State Departments of Archaeology, it is proposed to provide adequate tourist facilities at the major centres of cultural interest in a planned manner in coordination with the other concerned agencies including the State Governments.

6.3.2 The intention is to fully exploit the rich heritage of archaeological monuments and religious centres dear to the followers of various religions of the world as well as the rich heritage in the field of performing arts, the variety of which could itself be the sole objective of the tourist's visit to India.

Tourism – A Common Endeavour

7. While broadly the promotion of international tourism will be mainly the responsibility of the Central sector, and that of domestic tourism primarily of the State sector, the Centre would play a coordinating role supplementing the State effort wherever necessary. Further, tourism development cannot solely be the responsibility of the Government. It has to be a common endeavour of all the agencies vitally concerned with its development at Central and State levels, of public sector undertakings and the private sector, of airlines, railways and communications systems, municipal and local bodies, and educational and cultural organisations.

This combined effort will be directed towards achieving a comprehensive, well-rounded and integrated development enabling tourism to make a positive and effective contribution to the economic growth of the country.

Impact of Tourism

8.1 While the overall impact of tourism on a national scale may be difficult to measure as it is a pervasive activity rather than a tangible commodity, it can be more easily assessed in specific situations where the parameters can be more precisely defined. For example, the cost /benefit study of the Gulmarg Winter Sports Project has shown that the net social benefit accruing from winter sports development as envisaged would be around Rs. 600 crores over a period of 25 to 30 years, the multiplier effect being 3.3. In a similar study of the Kovalam Beach Resort Project, the multiplier effect was found to be 2.5. In the field of international tourism, foreign exchange earned from tourism in 1979-80 showed an increase of 20.4 per cent as against an increase of 12.8 per cent growth rate in the commodity exports from India. The Committee on Export Strategy — 1980s* in its report mentions that while India's exports altogether constituted 0.42 per cent of the total world exports in 1979, India's share of the world tourism receipts was 0.58 per cent. This was despite the fact that 1979 was one of the poorest years for tourism to India. These figures were as follows : 0.58 per cent in 1979; 0.64 per cent in 1980 and 0.76 per cent in 1981. The fact thus remains that given the opportunity tourism can make an effective contribution towards reducing the country's deficits in international trade. Equally, it can bring sizeable socio-economic benefits to those regions of the country which are rich in tourism potential.

8.2 Increasing attention will be given to regional tourism, *i.e.* the tourism among the countries of the South Asian Region (comprising the Indian subcontinent) extending the scope to cover Afghanistan, Iran and the Republic of Maldives. Through promotion of tourism in the region, tourism will attempt to play its role in bringing about greater understanding among the countries of the region and consciousness of the oneness of the region.

---

* This Committee was constituted by Government of India, Ministry of Commerce, Civil Supplies and Cooperation (Department. of Commerce) vide Resolution No. 4(23)79-EPL dated 28th June, 1979. Final Report was submitted in December, 1980.

Plan of Action

9.1 Thus, in order to maximise the benefits of tourism it will be necessary to have a selective approach for determining investment priorities. Rather than spread the resources thin and thereby dilute the impact of tourism, priority will be given to schemes which yield economic returns and generate social benefits. The development of tourist infrastructure will thus be taken up based on the 'travel circuit' concept in a 5 to 10 year perspective. This will enable intensive development of selected centres, dispel the tendency to concentrate in a few urban centres, and encourage the diversification of tourist attractions, particularly in opening up economically backward areas which hold many tourist attractions such as archaeological and historical monuments, places of natural beauty, festivals, arts and crafts.

9.1.2 To involve the youth of the country in national integration and make tourism a vehicle for achieving this objective, youth hostel activity will be given significant importance in the plan of action. This will facilitate the youth from different parts of the country exchanging views and ideas getting themselves exposed to the various parts of the country and thus bringing about greater understanding between youths of all parts of the country, apart from catalysing international understanding through the youth movement. The existing modest network of youth hostels set up for the purpose will be expanded and the movement strengthened substantially.

9.1.3 The policy on tourism will take cognizance of the need to underscore the fact that tourism facilities for the lower middle class and the poorer sections of the society for getting to know about other parts of the country through travel require to be augmented and towards this purpose, and with particular reference to pilgrimage tourism, cheap accommodation is proposed to be provided through *dharamshalas*, sarais, etc. making use of suitable organisations like the Bhartiya Yatri Avas Vikas Samiti and the like to put up such facilities.

9.2 Marketing strategy will be to broaden the tourist base in existing markets, explore new tourist markets, and promote and facilitate intra-regional travel, particularly from neighbouring countries. A dynamic and pragmatic approach will be adopted in identifying regions from where tourist traffic to India has growing potentiality as for instance, West Asian as well as North African countries where as a result of oil, there is a great boom and prosperity resulting in people in these countries desiring to go on pleasure tours abroad. These WANA countries have a predilection towards India because of its close link with West Asia and North Africa from historical times. Special emphasis has to be given for travel from these countries to India. The infrastructure will be so developed as to cater to the tastes of the tourists from these regions. Similarly, the infrastructure at Buddhist centres is being developed as for instance, through a series of Buddhist oriented hotels with a view to attracting large scale Buddhist traffic through charter as well as by the normal services to India making India a Buddhist destination. With the vast Buddhist population in the Far East, there is considerable potential for traffic to India from these countries. The assistance of the Railway Ministry is being sought for operating special charter trains to cover the Buddhist centres and also supplement accommodation in hotels through these special trains which would be self-contained mobile hotels, as it were.

9.3 Special attention will be paid to developing social tourism to benefit the weaker sections of society.

9.4 Manpower development and training will be given due weightage to ensure efficient service and effective management of tourist facilities for maximising returns on investments made.

9.5.1 To attract private sector investment in building up the tourist infrastructure and for augmenting various services to keep pace with the tourist demand, it will be necessary to extend fiscal and other incentives to the various segments of the tourism industry on par with those given to other export-oriented industries.

9.5.2 Towards this purpose every endeavour will be made to secure fiscal and other incentives from the concerned Ministries of Government in order to make investment in the tourism industry worthwhile. In this process an endeavour will also be made to highlight the fact that in the context of the country needing substantial foreign exchange for its developmental activities, tourism industry will constitute a major agency/industry for the acquisition of foreign exchange of a sizeable quantum not incomparable to, and in due course expect to exceed, the contribution of foreign exchange generated by the engineering goods industries, handloom and handicrafts industries and other major foreign exchange earning export-oriented industries.

9.5.3 In this context an endeavour will also have to be made to obtain for the tourism industry the status of an export-oriented industry.

Conservation and Development

10. A major consideration of tourism development will be to preserve our cultural and natural heritage which constitutes the major tourism resources of the country. Despoliation of the natural environment of archaeological monuments, beaches, mountains and places of natural beauty, disruption in the ecosystems of environmentally sensitive regions through haphazard growth of tourist facilities and injecting tourist inflow beyond the absorption capacity of the place/region, destruction of traditions in the culturally sensitive areas, clandestine selling of antiques and vandalism-are some of the negative aspects of tourism which can lead to the depletion of tourism resources of the country. Similarly, the environmental aspects of industrial, urban and other types of development, whether in the immediate vicinity of archaeological sites and places of natural beauty or in their peripheral areas are a matter of deep concern as they can adversely affect the development of tourism. A judicious balance, therefore, needs to be maintained between conservation and development. Appropriate measures therefore would be necessary to educate the people in appreciating their rich heritage, and eliciting their cooperation in preserving and protecting it.

New Ethos and Value

11. India has a long tradition of social and cultural values, and possesses a spiritual quality that has come down unbroken from time immemorial. It is this quintessence of our culture that tourism should be able to project so as to give to our people a sense of unity and identity, a broadening of their intellectual, emotional and cultural horizon and a sense of belonging and pride, and for the international traveller, tourism should create a better understanding of our land, people and culture. The cultural, social and economic benefits of tourism that flow from this policy should give a new ethos and value to tourism, and a new sense of purpose and direction to its development and promotion.

Conclusion

12. It is our earnest hope that this policy on tourism, being presented for the first time, will find wide acceptance and will help to enrich our life and bring greater prosperity to our people in the years to come.

APPENDIX-II

The National Action Plan for Tourism

Ministry of Civil Aviation and Tourism,
Government of India,
May 1992

Tourism has today, emerged as the fastest growing industry in the world. In 1990, the number of world travellers was 429 million who spent over US $ 249 billion. Direct employment in the industry was 112 million persons and indirect much more. While accurate statistics are not available, the figure of domestic tourists in the country was estimated at 62.3 million during 1990. Tourist arrivals in the country during the same period were 1.71 million, earning for the country Rs. 2440 crores in foreign exchange. During 1991-92 foreign exchange earnings are provisionally estimated at Rs. 3300 crores. The tourism industry in India generated in 1989-90 direct employment of 5.5 million persons and another 8 million who were employed indirectly. Given these dimensions of international tourism and the potential which exists in the country, there is tremendous scope for accelerated growth of tourism industry in the country.

OBJECTIVES

2. The objectives of the new Action Plan for Tourism are delineated below :

(a) *Socio-economic development of areas*

Tourism conferred considerable socio-economic benefits to the community thereby uplifting the quality of life. It can further foster development even in areas where other economic activities would be difficult to sustain.

(b) *Increasing employment opportunities*

Tourism industry generates employment, directly and indirectly, for about 13-14 million persons. Employment opportunities should be at least double the present level before the turn of the century.

(c) *Developing domestic tourism especially for the budget category*

Domestic tourists form the bulk of world tourist traffic. In India also, facilities for domestic tourists will be improved and expanded particularly the budget category so as to ensure an affordable holiday for them.

(d) *Preservation of national heritage and environment*

Tourism would be developed in a manner that our cultural expression and heritage are preserved in all its manifestations including support to arts and crafts. Preservation and enrichment of environment should also form an integral part of tourism development.

(e) *Development of international tourism and optimisation of foreign exchange earnings*

International tourism contributes substantially to foreign exchange earnings and keeping in view the country's requirements, tourism will be so developed that foreign exchange earnings increase from Rs. 2440 crores to Rs. 10,000 crores by the end of the century.

(f) *Diversification of the tourism product*

While retaining the traditional image of cultural tourism that India enjoys, diversification of the tourism product would continue, particularly in the field of leisure, adventure, convention and incentive tourism, thereby responding to the changing consumer needs.

(g) *Increase in India's share in world tourism*

Presently the foreign tourist arrivals in India constitute only about 0.4 per cent of the total foreign tourists' movement all over the world. One of the objectives of the action plan would be to increase India's share to 1 per cent within the next five years.

STRATEGY FOR DEVELOPMENT

3. The strategy for achieving the objectives is outlined below :
   - Improvement of tourism infrastructure.
   - Developing areas on a selective basis for integrated growth along with marketing of destinations to ensure optimal use of existing infrastructure.
   - Restructuring and strengthening the institutions for development of human resources.
   - Evolving a suitable policy for increasing foreign tourist arrivals and foreign exchange earnings.

IMPROVEMENT OF TOURIST INFRASTRUCTURE

4. The State has made substantial contribution in the service sector which is best left to private initiative and investment. The policy now would be to encourage private investment, both domestic and foreign, for accelerated growth. The role of Ministry of Tourism would be to conceptualise and deal with policy issues mainly.

Accommodation

5. Hotels form an important and vital segment of the tourism infrastructure in the country. It has been estimated that the present capacity of 44,405 hotel rooms in the approved category needs to be at least doubled in the next three years. The Government has already initiated steps in this direction. Fiscal concessions had been given under Section 80 HHD of the Income Tax Act whereby 50 per cent of the income earned on account of the foreign exchange earnings of a hotel are exempt from income tax and the remaining 50 per cent also exempt if reinvested in the tourism industry. This has had a positive impact on the pace of growth of hotels. However, this trend is particularly noticeable in metropolitan cities and commercial cities than in tourist destinations *per se*. In order to stimulate growth at tourist places also, the Government has given a concession that hotels set up in rural areas, hill stations, pilgrim centres and specified tourist destinations will be exempt from expenditure tax and 50 per cent of income tax for ten years.

6. The Government is also giving an interest subsidy on loans for construction of hotels. It is 1 per cent for loans up to 75 lakhs for 4-5 star

hotels and 3 per cent for all other approved hotels. *The interest subsidy to all 4-5 star hotels and all hotels in the metropolitan cities will now be discontinued. In special areas and specified destinations, however, the interest subsidy will be increased to 5 per cent for all 1, 2 and 3 star hotels to stimulate their growth.*

7. There are a large number of palaces, big and small, and *havelies* which can be very conveniently converted into hotels. Many of these are in a state of disrepair and their conversion into hotels will assist in preservation of this national heritage. It has, therefore, been decided to encourage the growth of these heritage hotels. In relaxation of their norms, the Tourism Finance Corporation of India will now advance loans for heritage hotel projects of Rs. 50 lakhs and above. *The Government will also give an interest subsidy of 5 per cent on loans advanced for construction of new Heritage hotels. A new scheme will be launched whereby this category of hotels will also be given a capital subsidy of Rs. 5 lakhs or 25 per cent of the cost, whichever is less.* For *havelis* located in rural areas, there is an added incentive of 10 year holiday from expenditure tax and 50 percent from income tax. It is hoped that these concessions will spur a rapid growth of heritage hotels in the country.

Encouraging Domestic Tourism

8. Measures are afoot to facilitate domestic tourism. *A new scheme for development of camping sites will be started specially for the low budget tourists.* Central assistance is being provided to enable State Tourism Development Corporations investing in tented accommodation and other facilities necessary for setting up adventure camps. *A scheme of Paying guest accommodation will also be introduced in as many places as possible to provide affordable and hygienic accommodation, both for domestic and foreign tourists. Similarly, classification rules will be suitably altered to recognise apartment hotels as these also provide affordable holidays to the domestic tourists. Further, rules will be amended to provide for recognition to tour operators engaged in domestic tourism. In fact, it will be prescribed that all recognised tour operators/travel agents do a certain percentage of their turnover in domestic tourism.* These measures will, no doubt, give a fillip to growth of low-budget tourism.

Pilgrim Tourism

9. *Pilgrim flows account for a very large percentage of domestic tourism.* Infrastructure facilities for tourists for pilgrim centres need to be substantially improved. *For this purpose, the Central Government will earmark a sum of Rs. 5.00 crores as Central assistance every year to enable State Tourism Development Corporations/private entrepreneurs to set up or improve accommodation facilities, way side amenities and transport systems at important pilgrim centres.*

Crafts Villages

10. The Surajkund Crafts Mela and Shilpgram, Udaipur, have been a tremendous draw with the tourists. Looking at the success of these centres, the Department *intends to set up crafts villages in different parts of the country and provide a boost to the traditional handicrafts of these regions.*

Fairs and Festivals

11. The fairs and festivals not only reflect the vast cultural heritage of India but have over the years become big attractions for tourists. These have been identified by the Ministry of Tourism and assistance given to develop and publicise them to attract even foreign tourists. Fairs like Pushkar Fair, Sonepur Cattle Fair, Kite Festival, Alleppey Boat Race, Dussehra Festival in Mysore and Kulu and others have already become a big attraction for tourists. *Ministry will give liberal financial assistance to develop these traditional fairs and festivals all over the country and promote them aggressively in the international markets.*

India's rich culture and heritage has been one of the major attractions for the international tourists who visit our country to experience different cultures, traditions and customs. At important tourist centres there are no structured arrangements for organising cultural evenings which could provide an experience or a glimpse of Indian culture to the visiting foreign tourists. *It will be the endeavour of the Government to have a tie-up with the zonal Cultural Centres for making arrangements at important tourist destinations to organise cultural evenings, son-et-lumieres, craft bazaars, food plazas and fairs and festivals all round the year.* Such activities will be organised in coordination with the Department of Culture and Archaeological Survey of India.

Road Transport

12. The other important segment of tourist infrastructure is road transport. The Government will be importing coaches for Buddhist circuit in Uttar Pradesh and Bihar as also 300 air conditioned units for the travel trade at concessional duties over the next two years. This will ensure that the tourist coaches are adequately equipped to meet the needs of the tourists. It is recognised that international quality luxury coaches/cars are essential for facilitating tourist movement to different parts of the country. Unfortunately, most of the existing transport units are now old and have outlived the utility needing to be replaced. *Government will introduce some suitable scheme by which this important felt need in tourism can be fulfilled.*

Travel Trade

13. Travel agents and tour operators constitute an important segment of tourism industry. Looking to the size of the country, it is imperative to encourage the travel trade in such a fashion that more and more people could come within the fold of travel trade. *It would be the endeavour of the Government to streamline and liberalise rules and procedures for recognising travel agents and tour operators.*

Facilitating tourist movement

14. Government has announced liberalised charter policy and the Director General (Civil Aviation) automatically grants permission expeditiously for charter flights in keeping with the guidelines prescribed. Charter flights have significantly added to tourism traffic to the country and it is hoped that they will be disbursed to tourism destinations in different parts of the country. The recently introduced air taxi scheme will augment the efforts of the national carriers and facilitate movement of tourists within the country. Foreign tourists are greatly attracted to travelling by the Railways and the Palace-on-Wheels in Rajasthan has been an unqualified success. *Government has recently announced a new tourist train on the lines of the Palace-on-Wheels to operate in the coming tourist season between Goa and Mysore.* Efforts will also be made to encourage tourist movement by water transport. The private sector will be encouraged to introduce cruises both river runs and along the coastal stretches.

Foreign Investment

15. 'Hotels and Tourism related industry' have been listed at item 4 in Appendix-III of the new Industrial Policy which provided for automatic approval of foreign investment in equity up to 51 per cent. With this liberalisation, it is imperative that special efforts are made to attract foreign investment in the tourism sector. The Government has set up a Committee under the chairmanship of the Principal Secretary to the Prime Minister to negotiate with parties abroad for investment in the country. Another *Sub-Committee to service this main Committee will be set up in this Ministry chaired by Secretary (Tourism) to obtain and concretise foreign investment in the tourism sector.*

Convention Tourism

16. Convention and conference tourism has assumed a great significance. In order to encourage convention tourism it would be desirable to set up fully integrated convention complexes in the country so that more and more international conferences and conventions could be attracted to India. *It would be the endeavour of the Government to set up a convention city with all facilities of international standards.*

DEVELOPING AREAS ON A SELECTIVE BASIS FOR INTEGRATED GROWTH

17. Hitherto Central assistance for development of tourism infrastructure to the States has been spread thinly over a large number of schemes/projects. Consequently, the desired level of development in places which have high potential has not taken place. Given this scenario, it has been decided that instead of spreading resources thinly, only special circuits/destinations will be taken up for intensive development. *In the first instance Government has identified 15 circuits/destinations for concentrated development both through Central assistance and investment by State Governments/private sector. These circuits are listed at Annexure- I.* As and when these circuits/destinations reach the prescribed level of development, new circuits/destinations could be added so that there is a uniform spread of tourist facilities in different parts of the country.

18. *The Government in conjunction with selected State Governments also proposes to notify a few Special Tourism Areas for integrated*

development of tourism facilities. The proposed Special Tourism Areas will be similar to the scheme of setting up notified Export Processing Zones designed to give a fillip to industries catering to export production. The selected Special Tourism Areas would have identifiable boundaries notified by the State Governments where land would be allotted for hotels and tourism related industries at concessional rates to prospective investors according to the Master Plan prepared. A Special Area Development Authority would be constituted by the State Governments to administer the Special Tourism Area with full delegation of powers under different statutes of the State Government. The Special Area Development Authority would prepare the Master Plan for the area and provide single window clearance facility to the investors. The State Government would provide basic infrastructure in terms of roads, transport, bus terminals, wayside amenities, electrical grids, water supply, law and order and municipal services. The Central Government would provide infrastructural support such as airports and airline services, railway stations, communications network and post/telegraph/banking services. Both the Central and State Governments would grant exemption from specified Central/State Taxes and freeze rates on water and electric supply for at least 10 years in order to attract investments.

19. The scheme for setting up of select Special Tourism Areas was approved in a resolution adopted by the Conference of State Tourism Ministers held in New Delhi on 10th December, 1991. A copy of the Resolution adopted is at *Annexure-II.*

The selection of Special Tourism Areas would be done by the Central Government in consultation with those State Governments who are willing to offer the maximum facilities for the successful functioning of such Special Tourism Areas.

Special efforts will be made to attract foreign investment in these areas.

20. *A scheme for giving Assistance for Specified Tourism Areas (ASTA) will be started to provide financial assistance for equity and other tourism related activities in such areas as are specified by the Government.*

21. *The Government will lay special emphasis on the development of island tourism in places such as the Andamans and Lakshadweep.* A decision has recently been taken to selectively open out some of the islands

for tourism purposes. This will be done keeping in mind the carrying capacity and the need to preserve the environment. The emphasis will be on high value low volume tourism traffic to the selected islands and the facilities to be provided would blend with the natural beauty of the islands.

RESTRUCTURING AND STRENGTHENING INSTITUTIONS FOR MANPOWER DEVELOPMENT

22. At present there are 15 institutions of Hotel Management and Catering Technology and 16 Foodcraft Institutes in the country. The combined turnover of trained personnel is estimated at 8,500 in the accommodation and hospitality sector as against the annual requirement of 28,000 trained personnel. The Government will; therefore, restructure and strengthen the training programme to meet this shortfall.

23. The Foodcraft Institutes which provide general training to the students have served a useful purpose in the initial years. There is an urgent need to supplement these activities with certain specialised Institutes like Chef Training Institutes. *A National Culinary Institute will be set up to meet the requirements of trained manpower in the country and the region.*

24. The Institutes of Hotel Management and Catering Technology have fulfilled an important need and students from these Institutes find ready employment in the hotel industry. However, a survey has shown that these students take up jobs mainly in the metros. Consequently the hotel industry in the smaller places does not get trained manpower. *To correct this imbalance, regional institutes would be set up. Students will be admitted on regional basis and encouraged to take up jobs in these areas.*

25. The Indian Institute of Tourism and Travel Management will be strengthened both in staff and equipment to become the premier institution for providing trained manpower for the travel trade in the country. National universities will also be involved in this effort and would be given financial and other assistance for introducing tourism courses in the country.

MARKETING AND OVERSEAS PUBLICITY

26. In the field of marketing and overseas publicity, the Department will coordinate its activities with Air-India and other agencies operating in foreign countries to obtain optimum results. Emphasis will now be on

direct promotion by way of going directly to the consumer. Familiarisation tours; joint promotion with departmental stores and other organizations; and assistance to tour operators promoting India will constitute the major planks of the publicity strategy.

The marketing of India as a generalised destination has obvious drawbacks since foreign travellers do not get indepth focus of local tourist attractions. A major change in strategy is specific destination marketing which concentrates on specified circuits/destinations in the overseas publicity programme. This year, for example, through special concentration on South India, tourism flows were increased by almost 35 per cent to South Indian destinations and helped diversify tourism away from the traditional destinations.

In many countries tourism trade fairs have become an annual feature where different segments of tourism industry inter act with one another and the tourism product is sold to wholesalers and retailers. Often a large number of consumers also participate in such trade fairs. In order to promote tourism to India *a tourism trade fair could be held once in three years where the indigenous industry and foreign travel agents/tour operators could fruitfully interact.*

The Government have introduced tourist information service — TOURNET in their domestic offices and certain selected countries. *It is proposed to make available a computerised multi-lingual tourist information service which could be installed at different outlets like airports, hotels and trade counters apart from the tourist offices of Government of India.* The service could give instant information on mode of transport, food, accommodation, places of interest and cost of services in different languages to the tourists visiting the country.

SUMMARY OF THE ACTION PLAN

27. Based on the prescriptions contained in the foregoing paragraphs, a summary outline of the Action Plan for Tourism proposed to be implemented, is indicated in the subsequent paragraphs.

28. The items which pertain to the Ministry of Tourism are as below:

(a) Creation of Special Tourism Areas as notified zones for intensive investment and development.

(b) Starting the scheme for giving Assistance for Specified Tourism Areas (ASTA) for providing finances for tourism and tourism related industry in specified areas/circuits.

(c) Special category of Heritage hotels/health resorts to be created and provided
- technical/consultancy help,
- loans from financial institutions,
- interest subsidy,
- marketing and operational expertise.

(d) Tourist trains to be started on important tourist routes based on the success of the Palace-on-Wheels.

(e) River cruises to be operated in specified circuits.

(f) Revamping of foreign offices to make them more accountable in terms of specified targets.

(g) Information revolution; information system to be revamped to provide positive projection of India in all leading markets.

(h) Special airline/hotel packages for selected tourist destinations.

(i) Provision of information counter for airlines, trains, hotels, tourist information at major international airports.

29. Items which pertain to other ministries :-

(a) Tourist facilities at major international airports like
- immigration,
- customs,
- luggage,
- money changing facilities,
- airport coaches/taxis.

(b) Liberalized charters through announced policy and automatic clearance.

(c) Open sky policy for routes on which Air-India does not operate or operates in a limited fashion.

Annexure - I

CIRCUITS-CUM-DESTINATIONS IDENTIFIED FOR INTENSIVE DEVELOPMENT

Travel Circuits

1. Kulu–Manali–Leh
2. Gwalior–Shivpuri–Orchha–Khajuraho
3. Bagdogra–Sikkim–Darjeeling–Kalimpong
4. Bhubaneswar–Puri–Konark
5. Hyderabad–Nagarjunasagar–Tirupati
6. Madras–Mamallapuram–Pondicherry
7. Rishikesh–Narender Nagar–Gangotri–Badrinath
8. Indore–Ujjain–Maheshwar–Omkareshwar–Mandu
9. Jaisalmer–Jodhpur–Bikaner–Barmer

Destinations

1. Lakshadweep Islands
2. Andaman Islands
3. Manali (Solang–Nalah)
4. Bekal Beach
5. Muttukadu Beach
6. Kangra (Pong Dam)

Annexure - II

RESOLUTIONS ADOPTED BY THE STATE TOURISM MINISTERS' CONFERENCE ON 10TH DECEMBER 1991 AT NEW DELHI

The State Tourism Ministers met on 10th December, 1991 under the chairmanship of Union Minister of Civil Aviation and Tourism, Shri Madhavrao Scindia, with a view to providing a major boost for development of tourism in the country. Consequent to the detailed discussions on various issues, the following recommendatory resolutions were made :

SPECIAL TOURISM AREA

(a) The State Governments should consider development of Special Tourism Areas in consultation with the Ministry of Tourism, Government of India.
   - Prior approval of the Ministry of Tourism will have to be sought before actual implementation of the project.
   - The Special Tourism Areas will have identifiable boundaries to be notified by the State Governments.
   - Land would be allotted for hotels and tourism related industry at concessional rates to prospective investors according to the Master Plan prepared.

(b) In each Special Tourism Area, a Special Area Development Authority would be constituted by the State Governments.
   - With full delegation of powers under different statutes of the State Government.
   - Provide single window clearance facility to the investors.
   - The authority would prepare a Master Plan within 6 months for development of Special Tourism Areas.

(c) The State Government should provide basic infrastructure in terms of roads, transport network, bus terminals, wayside amenities, electrical grids, water supply, law and order and municipal services.

(d) The State Governments should freeze the rates on water and electricity supply at least for 10 years in such areas.

(e) The State Governments should exempt all projects connected with hotels and tourism related industry being set up in the Special Tourism Areas from all State and local body taxes for a period of at least 10 years.

(f) The Central Government should provide infrastructural support as required for development of Special Tourism Areas such as :
- Airports and airline services
- Railway stations
- Communication network
- Post/telegraph services/banks.

(g) The Central Government should consider granting exemption from specific central taxes, and providing fiscal incentives in the shape of capital subsidy, interest subsidy, etc., for development of capital intensive tourism projects.

(h) The Central Government should set up a **Tourism Development Fund** for providing equity support to investors in such areas for capital intensive projects.

(i) The Central Government should provide special clearance for all projects being set up in Special Tourism Areas from the environmental angle.

(j) India Investment Centre/Embassies/Government of India Tourist Offices to give wide publicity of such areas to foreign investors.

(k) At National level a Coordination Committee should be set up with representatives from the State Governments, private trade and the Government of India for coordinating all matters related to the Special Tourism Areas.

APPENDIX-III

Draft
National Tourism Policy

1997

Draft National Tourism Policy

1. *The Preamble*

In the context of economic liberalisation and globalisation being pursued by the country, the development policies of no sector can remain static. It is particularly so in the case of tourism which involves the activities of human beings travelling to and staying in places outside their usual environment for the purpose of education, experience, enrichment and enjoyment. In addition, the emergence of tourism as an important instrument for sustainable human development including poverty alleviation, employment generation, environmental regeneration and advancement of women and other disadvantaged groups in the country apart from promoting social integration and international understanding also necessiated the enunciation of a new pragmatic tourism policy. Further, travel has become an important social phenomenon of the modern society entailing demand on various facilities and services including transport, accommodation, restaurants, entertainment facilities, shopping outlets and sites of tourist attractions and thereby activising a process of accelerated economic production and distribution. The enterprises/establishments engaged in such wide-ranging diverse activities to meet the tourist demand constitute the tourism industry which needs to be recognised and developed by providing the required policy support.

2. *Growth and Structure of Tourism in India*

2.1 Tourism Resources

India's tourism resources are immense. Its historic and cultural mosaic is unique. The monuments, sculptures and paintings of India bear testimony to the national ethos for harmony and diversities to be reflected in a composite whole. The geographical features of India are bothe colourful and varied. The lofty Himalayas inspire human spirit to divine heights and offer opportunities for a whole range of adventure sports. Some of the beaches in India are the best in the world with an irresistible combination of sun, sand and sea. The wealth of eco-systems consisting of biosphere reserves, mangroves, coral reefs, deserts, mountains and forests along with the flora and fauna provide enormous potential for eco-tourism. Above all, India is a country of numerous fairs and festivals as well as arts and handicrafts which represent the mystical lifestyles of Indian society. These attractions of India hold virtually an unlimited potential for tourism development.

2.2 Tourism since Independence

Though India had a good amount of tourism activity when it became independent 50 years ago, it did not figure in the Constitution of India except that some of its components were mentioned in the Central or State lists. There was also no allocation for tourism development during First Five Year Plan. Tourism became a constituent of planning process during Second Five Year Plan (1956-61) with a token allocation of Rs. 3.36 crores for both Central and State sectors put together. The developmental approach during Second Plan was mainly on creating isolated facilities in important tourist centres. The Third-Plan witnessed the beginning of an era for the development of activities connected with tourism, particularly adventure tourism by the establishment of 'Winter Sports Complex' at Gulmarg in Jammu and Kashmir. The India Toursim Development Corporation (ITDC) was also set up in 1966 to develop tourism infrastructure and promote India as a tourist destination.

The approach during Fourth and Fifth Plans was expansion and improvement of tourist facilities with a view to promote 'destination traffic' as distinct from 'transit traffic'. Integrated development of selected tourist centres like Kovalam, Gulmarg, Goa, Kullu-Manali, etc., received much attention and became the symbolic models of resort tourism in India.

The Sixth Plan (1980-85) was a major landmark in the history of Indian tourism. The first ever 'Tourism Policy' of the country was announced during 1982 which specified the development objectives and provided an action plan based on 'travel circuit' concept to maximise the benefits of tourism.

The development of tourism was stated as a plan objective during Seventh Plan (1985-90) and the sector was accorded the status of an industry. It thus became a watershed plan for Indian tourism. The National Committee on Tourism set up by the Government in 1986 to evaluate the economic and social relevance of tourism in India and to draw up a long-term plan for its development submitted its report in 1988 and recommended a number of measures for ensuring accelerated growth of tourism. On the basis of these recommendations a package of incentives was made available for tourism industries and the 'Tourism Finance Corporation (TFCI)' was set up to finance tourism projects.

The development plan for tourism during the Eighth Plan (1992-97) was based on the 'National Action Plan for Tourism' presented in the Parliament on 5th May, 1992. It proposed to achieve diversification of tourism products, accelerated growth of tourism infrastructure, effective marketing and promotional efforts in the overseas markets and removal of all impediments to tourism. A major component of the Action Plan was the development of all inclusive 'Special Tourism Areas' and intensive development of selected circuits. The Action Plan did not specify the infrastructural requirements and the investments needed to meet the targets and the sources of funding for the same. The 'Tourism Synergy Programme' enlisting the activities and infrastructural components to be provided by various agencies including the private sector and State Governments was thus prepared in 1993. It was further modified and converted into a 'National Strategy for the Development of Tourism' during 1996. These documents were aimed at achieving a greater realisation of the importance of tourism, a consensus on the developmental needs, positive contribution of all the infrastructural departments in a co-ordinated manner, higher plan allocations and introduction of new schemes for accelerated development of tourism.

2.3 Domestic Tourism

Travel for pilgrimage and learning has been an integral part of Indian culture ever since the beginning of its civilization. Several centres of learning and religious worship developed all over the country since ancient times. This gave further impetus to the mass movement of people from one place to another. Development of traditional industries and trade created the stream of business travellers. Several trading routes were established and traders started frequenting the centres of trade from distant places. The ancient rulers gave due recognition to these travellers and created many wayside facilities like inns, *sarais, dharamshalas* and caravans for their benefit. These formed the tourism infrastructure of India in those days. Thus, India has been experiencing massive movement of domestic tourists for several centuries.

A few centuries ago the Moghul rulers built luxurious palaces and enchanting gardens in places of natural scenic attraction. During the period of British rule in India, domestic tourism received a new direction and meaning due to the establishment of Railways and export/import houses at port towns introducing qualitative and quantitative changes in the Indian business tourism. In addition, the construction of circuit houses, dak bungalows and forest lodges provided the infrastructure for leisure and wildlife tourism. Several hill stations were also developed during the period which became the core of Indian leisure tourism. The emergence of a large 'urban middle class' coupled with better transport and communication facilities has created a new class of holiday and leisure tourists in contemporary India. The National Action Plan for Tourism, 1992 thus gave considerable emphasis on the development of domestic tourism inclulding pilgrim tourism. Thus, domestic tourism has become the mainstay of Indian tourism and it is likely to grow substantially during the coming years. The economic, social and cultural advantages of domestic tourism are:

- Domestic movement of people for non-migratory purposes constitutes shifts in consumer markets of variable importance and are catalysts of the national economy.
- It has extremely high social, cultural, educational and political value and true economic value, although still embryonic in some cases.
- It generates large-scale employment opportunities particularly in rural areas and restrains the exodus of people to large towns.
- The new jobs created to meet the needs of domestic tourists have a relatively low unit cost per job and it helps increase the number of jobs.
- Production methods for services demanded by domestic tourists generally remain simple and based on local materials.

- It also requires only simple installations and infrastructure in transport, accommodation and catering which would take into account local, cultural, political and historic traditions.
- It has the ability to sustain and maintain the tourism industry during lean periods of international toursim by providing an alternative for demand substitution.
- It contributes to an improved balancing of national economy thorugh redistribution of national income and thus provides a better environment for the growth of both domestic and inbound tourism.
- It is the single unifying force which helps to achieve understanding between various linguistic, religious and communal groups living in different parts of the country. It thus contributes towards strengthening the fabric of national unity and cultural integration.

2.4. Inbound Tourism

Tourism is the world's largest export industry. In India also the foreign exchange earning from tourism is the third largest after readymade garments and gems & jewellery. Tourism receipts have been growing at a phenomenal rate in the recent years and it has become the single largest component of the services export. The projections available indicate that tourism would become the largest export industry in India too as it has already attained the top position in the world context. The other benefits of inbound tourism are:

- The projection of national image abroad, reduction of ideological gaps and enhancement of international understanding are generally better achieved through inbound tourism.
- Inbound tourism generates larger employment opportunities per tourist and leads to more income to local community.
- International tourists visiting interiors of the country for reasons of purity of environment and nature contribute to the development of such areas particularly in backward regions.
- Inbound tourism has significant linkages with the art and artefacts of the country including handicrafts and thus contributes to the improvement of living conditions of village artisans.

- Expansion of inbound tourism also leads to the provision of better infrastructural facilities in specific areas and thus stimulates diversification and development of other industries.

Though India achieved substantial growth in international tourist arrivals since 1951, the share of India in the world tourist traffic still remains to be less than 0.4 per cent. It is, however, encouraging to note that the average duration of stay of inbound tourists in India is one of the highest in the world. Considering the dimensions of the country and the multitude of attractions it possess, the potential of India in attracting international tourists is yet to be realised. The perceived constraints in the expansion of toursim are inadequate infrastructure including poor accessibility and non-availability of trained manpower in sufficient number.

2.5. Outbound Tourism

A large number of Indians go abroad every year for various purposes including business, study, pilgrimage, pleasure, etc. The process of economic liberalisation and growing affluence of people are likely to accelerate the outbound tourist traffic from India considerably. Though this aspect of tourism has not been the concern of the Department of Tourism so far, it has become necessay to recognise the phenomenon and evaluate its social and economic consequences. The volume of inbound traffic is also often linked to outbound tourism as international carriers have to depend on both for their operations.

3. *Objectives*

The national objectives of tourism development are :

(i) It becomes a unifying force nationally and internationally fostering better understanding through travel.

(ii) It gives a direction and opportunity to the people of the country through inbound, outbound and domestic tourism to understand the geographical and cultural diversity of nations and regions as well as the aspirations and viewpoints of others so as to bring about a greater national integration and cohesion.

(iii) It offers opportunities to the youth of the country not only for employment but also for taking up activities of nation-building character like sports, adventure and the like.

(iv) It brings socio-economic benefits to the community and the State in terms of faster economic growth, larger employment opportunities, better income generation and foreign exchange earning, balanced development of backward areas and weaker sections, higher tax revenue to the State and causes sustainable human development.

(v) It becomes a positive force for the preservation and enrichment of our cultural heritage in all its manifestations and causes accretion and strength rather than damage to our social and cultural values.

(vi) It should also become a reason for better preservation and protection of our natural resources, environment and ecology.

(vii) It should become a major avenue for the people of India and other counrites to see, feel and admire its magnificent attractions and achievements including natural beauty, geographical and cultural diversities, hertage of arts and crafts and industrial and scientific progress.

(viii) Above all, tourism should be able to project the quintessence of our culture so as to give our people a sense of unity and identity, a broadening of their intellectual, emotional and cultural horizon and a sense of belonging and pride and for the international traveller, tourism should create a better understanding of our land, people and culture.

4. *The Policy Framework*

The national policies with regard to tourism for achieving the objectives enumerated in this statment have to be consistent with the existing global scenario as well as national priorities and ethos. The policy should also take care of all possible conflicts and ensure sustained growth of tourism on desired lines. Taking into account these considerations, the following policy guidelines have been formulated.

4.1 Recognition

The economic and social benefits of tourism and its importance as an instrument of economic growth have to be fully recognised by all sections of the society. There is still a belief that the potential of the tourism would be determined by the income levels of inhabitants and is basically a leisure industry not requiring the attention of planners and administrators. This belief based on information gap has systematically constrained the development of tourism in the country over the years. ***It would, therefore, be the policy of the Goverenement to bridge this information gap through proper statistical documentation of the impact of tourism and its wide publicity to create awareness so that tourism is given due recognition and national priority.***

4.2 The Product

Persons travelling to other places invariably seek a pleasant and delectable experience on their trips. The most desired tourism product thus consists of :

- an environment of peace and stability;
- an assurance of safety and security;
- a friendly host society;
- an industry and a Governemnt that provide the requisite facilities promptly and efficiently;
- absence of extortion and hostility;
- accessible tourist attractions;
- an integrated system of physical infrastructure that does not fail—These include :
  - — international air seat capacity;
  - — internal transport system;
  - — hotels and restaurants of quality;
  - — entertainment and recreational avenues;
  - — shopping and communication facilities;
  - — well preserved monuments with tourist amenities;
  - — basic amenities like drinking water, toilets, refreshment centres, etc., at the tourist sites.

The policy, therefore, will be to work towards creating such a tourism product to the extent possible.

4.3 The Responsibility: A Multi-Dimensional Activity

Tourism consists of several goods and services consumed by the tourists at their places of visit. These are provided by a multitude of establishments and agencies functioning at various levels. Tourists also have to come into contact with various Government agencies and a numebr of infrastructural facilities are being provided by them. The development of tourism, therefore, cannot be the responsibility of any single agency. It is also not possible to have any artificial demarcation of responsibilities between the Central and State Governments as most of the delivery systems are primarily within the control of State/Union Territory Governments. ***The policy, therefore, will be to develop tourism as a common endeavour of all the agencies vitally concerned with it at the Central and State levels, public sector undertakings and the private sector.***

4.4 The Need for Co-ordination and Synergy

The infrastructure for tourism consists of not only the on-site facilities like hotels, restaurants, entertainment facilities, etc., but also includes all forms of transport and communications, infrastructure and basic amenities. The provisions of an integrated system of physical infrastructure including air, rail and water transport facilities, communication systems and basic amenities like electricity, water supply, drainage and solid waste disposal systems is a pre-requisite for the development of tourism in any area identified for the same. All the departments/agencies involved in infrastructure development have to, therefore, adopt a joint approach and establish synergy in the development of infrastructure for tourism. ***The policy, therefore, would be to ensure the necessary linkages and synergies in the policies and programmes of all such departments/agencies by establishing effective co-ordination mechanisms at Central, State and District levels.***

4.5 The Approach

Tourism Policy, 1982 envisaged a selective approach based on travel circuit concept in the provision of tourism infrastructure to achieve intensive development of selected centres. The National Action Plan for Tourism, 1992 also reiterated the need for such a policy to achieve significant impact on infrastructural develoment with the limited resources available. These policies, however, did not succeed in view of persistent demands for several small projects to meet the needs of domestic tourists in almost every place of tourist interest. Even the Government of India essentially followed a scheme approach instead of area approach in providing financial assistance for the development of tourism infrastructure. The approach for the future development of tourism has to, therefore, take into account both the needs for selective development and the demands of a wide cross-section of domestic tourists. ***The policy will be to encourage people's participation in tourism development including Panchayati Raj institutions, local bodies, non-governmental organisations and enterprising local youth to create public awareness and to achieve a wider spread of tourist facilities. The Central Government investment would be concentrated to large extent in centres selected for integrated development.***

4.6 The Choice

International tourist traffic to the country is largely confined to certain selected centres and destinations at present. There is also a fair level of seasonality in the international tourist arrivals. As a result there is a good deal of congestion and scarcity of facilities in some of these centres during peak seasons. The tourist traffic to some of the centres have even exceeded the carrying capacity with the attendant problem of environmental degradation. Even the metropolitan cities like Bombay and Delhi have started experiening scarcity of accommodation and other facilities in peak seasons. It has, therefore, become necessary to go beyond the beaten tracks and to facilitate direct visit of tourists to new destinations. However, the choice of such new destinations for development will have to be based on their intrinsic attractions, potential for development and the carrying capacity as well as availability of resources. ***The policy would be, therefore, to identify such destinations and work towards their integrated development with the involvement of all the infrastructural departments, State Governments and the private sector and to facilitate direct and easy access to those destinations.***

4.7 Forms of Tourism

The main strength of Indian tourism at present is its cultural attractions, particularly, the large number of monuments and archaeological remains scattered throughout the country, its art and artefacts and colourful fairs and festivals. The country is also endowed with a number of other tourist attractions and options including beach tourism, forests, wildlife and land- scapes for ecotourism, snow, river and mountain peaks for adventure tourism, health resources and farms for health tourism, technological parks and science museums for science tourism, centres of pilgrimage for spiritual tourism, etc. There are also facilities for conference and convention tourism and shopping tours. ***The policy, therefore, would be to diversify the tourism product in such a way that it supplements the mainstream of cultural tourism. It would also be ensured that the appropriate form of tourism based on specific features of attraction and ecological considerations is developed in each identified area.***

4.8 Levels of Development

The principle of sustainable development stipulates that the level of development does not exceed the carrying capacity of the area. ***The policy would be to ensure adherence to such limits through appropriate planning instruments, guidelines and enabling regulations.***

4.9 Role of the Government

Tourism is a multi-sectoral activity and the industry is affected by many other sectors of the national economy. The State has to, therefore, ensure intergovernmental linkages and co-ordination. It also has to play a pivotal role in tourism management and promotion, in particular, the Government has to :

(i) Provide public infrastructural facilities including local planning and zoning arrangements.

(ii) Plan tourism development as a part of the overall area development strategy.

(iii) Create nucleus infrastructure in the initial stages of development to demonstrate the potential of the area.

(iv) Provide support facilities and facilitation services to private enterprises along with appropriate incentives and land policies.

(v) Introduce regulatory measures to ensure social, cultural and environmental sustainability.

(vi) Ensure that the type and scale of tourism development is compatible with the environment and socio-cultural milieu of the area.

(vii) Ensure that the local community is fully involved and the benefits of tourism accrue to them.

(viii) Facilitate availability of trained manpower particularly from amongst the local population jointly with the industry.

(ix) Undertake research, prepare master plans, and facilitate formulation of marketing strategies.

(x) Organise overseas promotion and marketing jointly with the industry

(xi) Facilitate the growth of a dynamic tourism sector.

4.10 Role of Private Sector

As tourism has emerged as the largest export industry globally, the private sector has to consider investment in tourism from a long–term perspective and create the required facilities including accommodation, restaurants, entertainment facilities, shopping complexes, etc., in areas identified for tourism develoment. In general the private sector has to:

(i) Build and manage the required tourist facilities in all places of tourist interest.

(ii) Assume collective responsibility for laying down industry standards, ethics and fair practices.

(iii) Ensure preservation and protection of tourist attractions and give lead in green practices.

(iv) Involve the local community in tourism projects and ensure that the benefits of tourism accrue to them in right measure.

(v) Undertake industry training and manpower development to achieve excellence in quality of services.

(vi) Participate in the preparation of investment guidelines and marketing strategies and assist in database creation and research.

(vi) Ensure safety and security of tourists.

(viii) Endeavour to promote tourism on a sustained and long term perspective.

4.11 Facilitation Services

Tourists have to pass through several Government agencies so as to meet the requirements under various laws. These include obtaining visas, undergoing immigration checks, obtaining permits to visit certain areas, payment of fees for certain facilities, etc. ***The endeavour of the Government would be to improve efficiency in providing such facilitation services and make travel a pleasant experience.***

4.12 Foreign Investments and Incentives

In view of large investment requirements in the tourism sector and the need for maintaining high quality standards in services, hotels and tourism related industries will continue to be in the priority list of industries for foreign investment. ***Further, in order to offset the specific constraints of tourism industry and to put in place the required infrastructure as quickly as possible, particularly in less developed areas, appropriate incentive schemes would be considered. It would also be the endeavour of the Government to put in place uniform taxation and land policies in all the States/Union Territories.***

4.13 Resources for Development

Development of tourism to the extent desired would involve heavy investments in infrastructure. The resources for such investments have to come mostly from private investors, financial institutions and external borrowing. Financial viability and commercial returns are the guiding factors in such investments. Very often, it would depend on investments to bridge certain critical gaps in infrastructure which by itself may not be commercially remunerative. Special funds have to be, therefore, created for such investments. ***It would be thus the policy of the Government to facilitate larger flow of funds to tourism infrastructure and to create a Tourism Development Fund to bridge critical infrastructure gaps.***

4.14 Regions of Special Interest

The seven States of North East with beautiful landscapes, lush green forests, exotic wildlife, unique forms of art and culture and affable tribal societies have hitherto remained backward due to various reasons including poor infrastructure. These States along with other States in the Himalayan Region offer enormous potential for the development of ecotourism. Similarly the islands of Andaman and Nicobar as well as Lakshadweep are ideal for sustainable development of island tourism. It is also important to revive and strengthen tourism industry in Jammu and Kashmir to accelerate the economic growth of the State. ***It would, therefore, be the policy of the Government to initiate and support special programmes and schemes for the development of tourism in these regions with a view to achieve overall economic development of the region.***

4.15 Conservation and Development

Tourism development needs to be properly guided and regulated to avoid adverse impact on the natural environment and cultural heritage which constitute the tourist attraction. Despoilation of natural environment, archaeological monuments, beaches, mountains and places of natural beauty; disruption in the eco-system to environmentally sensitive regions; destruction of traditions in the culturally sensitive areas; clandestine selling of antiques and vandalism are some of the negative aspects of tourism. A judicious balance, therefore, needs to be maintained between conservation and development. ***The policy, therefore, would be to maintain balance through planning restrictions and by educating the people in appreciating their rich heritage and by eliciting their co-operation in preserving and protecting it.***

4.16 Adoption of New Technologies

The revolutionary changes that are taking place in the computer and communication technologies, and other relevant sectors would be adopted in the tourism sector to provide better facilities to tourists and to market the tourism product.

5. Plan of Action

The broad plan of action for the implementataion of the policies to achieve the objectives would consist of the following:

(i) Preparing an action plan specifying short, medium and long term strategies and the role of each of the players in the development of tourism.

(ii) Strengthening the statistical machinery, reporting systems, research and database on tourism to measure the economic and social benefits of tourism, identifying potential tourist destinations for integrated development, plan infrastructure development, formulating marketing strategies and monitoring the progress of implementation and impact of various programmes and projects.

(iii) Creating public awareness about economic and social benefits of tourism amongst administrators, planners and the masses through seminars, workshops, presentations, etc.

(iv) Launching of campaigns through local bodies, non-governmental organisations, youth centres, etc., to create awareness about the traditions of Indian hospitality and the importance of extending warmth and affection to tourists so as to control touting, extortion and harassment to tourists.

(v) Initiating measures for ensuring public participation by encouraging Panchayati Raj institutions, local bodies, religious trusts, etc., to achieve a wider spread of tourist facilities.

(vi) Strengthening the institutional set-up for human resources development and improving the standards of training in private institutes through accredition and quality control. It will include the setting up of an Advanced Institute of Hotel Management and a Culinary Institute apart from strengthening the existing training infrastructure.

(vii) Setting up a National Tourism Documentation Centre equipped with modern technology systems to function as repository of research findings and publications on tourism.

(viii) Setting up an advisory 'Board of Tourism Industry and Trade' to achieve effective co-ordination with other infrastructural departments and the private sector. Such institutions will also be promoted at the State and District levels.

(ix) Strengthening the existing organisational structure to make it possible to perform its multifarious activities efficiently for the development of tourism. Setting-up of a 'National Tourism Authority' will be considered in this regard.

(x) Giving guidance and financial assistance to State/Union Territory Governments for preparing Tourism Master Plans, identifying tourism resources, prioritising development circuits and projects and specifying the most suitable forms fo tourism.

(xi) Continuing to provide financial assistance to State/Union Territory Governments for developing various forms of tourism and tourism products and creating a 'Tourism Development Fund' to bridge infrastructural gaps.

(xii) Focussing on the development of ecotourism in the North East and other Himalayan States along with Andaman and Nicobar and Lakshadweep Islands and re-establishment of tourism industry in Jammu and Kashmir.

(xiii) Implementing integrated/intensive development of tourist destinations after assessing the carrying capacity, local aspirations and the benefits likely to accrue to the community.

(xiv) Preparing specific policies and guidelines for the development of each form of tourism and giving wide publicity to them. In particular, policies and guidelines for ecotourism development and guidlines for ensuring safety and security of adventure tourism will be formulated.

(xv) Imposing regulatory measures on developers, operators, tourists and the local communities under the existing laws and rules to ensure social, cultural and environmental sustainability of tourism projects.

(xvi) Providing an institutional mechanisam to deal with the complaints received from tourists and the industry so as to create a better security perception amongst actual and potential visitors.

(xvii) Providing the required assistances and facilitation services to both domestic and foreign investors for setting-up tourism projects. Efforts would also be made to set-up single window clearance mechanisms and to ensure uniform taxation and land policies in each of the State/Union Territories.

(xviii) Encouraging the private sector to create infrastructural facilities by providing suitable incentives on a selective basis. In particular, Heritage hotels, paying guest accommodation and development of mega tourism projects would be given priority.

(xix) Launching entrepreneurship development and self employment programmes to involve the educated youth in providing various tourist facilities and services and thereby creating employment opportunities.

(xx) Improving the efficiency of tourist facilitation services by co-ordinating with all the concerned agencies, adopting technological solutions and imparting training to functionaries at the cutting edge level like customs and immigration officials, taxi drivers and porters, guides, etc.

(xxi) Improving accessibility and promoting direct arrivals to the destinations of interest.

(xxii) Identifying potential tourism markets and segments and adopting focussed marketing strategies based on research to make promotional and marketing efforts cost effective.

(xxiii) Adopting new technologies like INTERNET and CD-ROMs in tourism promotion and marketing.

APPENDIX-IV

List of World Tourism Organisation (WTO) Member States

1. Afghanistan
2. Albania
3. Algeria
4. Andorra
5. Angola
6. Argentina
7. Armenia
8. Austria
9. Bangladesh
10. Benin
11. Bolivia
12. Bosnia and Herzegovina
13. Botswana
14. Brazil
15. Bulgaria
16. Burkina Faso
17. Burundi
18. Cambodia
19. Cameroon
20. Central Arfican Republic
21. Chad
22. Chile
23. China
24. Colombia
25. Congo
26. Costa Rica
27. Cote d'Ivoire
28. Croatia
29. Cuba
30. Cyprus
31. Czech Republic
32. Democratic People's
33. Democratic Republic
    Republic of Korea of the
    Congo
34. Djibouti
35. Dominican Republic
36. Ecuador
37. Egypt
38. El Salvador
39. Equatorial Guinea
40. Eritrea

41. Ethiopia
42. Fiji
43. Finland
44. France
45. Gabon
46. Gambia
47. Georgia
48. Germany
49. Ghana
50. Greece
51. Grenada
52. Guatemala
53. Guinea
54. Guinea-Bissau
55. Haiti
56. Hungary
57. India
58. Indonesia
59. Iran, Islamic Republic of
60. Iraq
61. Israel
62. Italy
63. Jamaica
64. Japan
65. Jordan
66. Kazakstan
67. Kenya
68. Kuwait
69. Kyrgyzstan
70. Lao People's Democratic
71. Lebanon Republic of
72. Lesotho
73. Libyan Arab Jamahiriya
74. Madagascar
75. Malawi
76. Malaysia
77. Maldives
78. Mali
79. Malta
80. Mauritania
81. Mauritius
82. Mexico
83. Mongolia
84. Morocco
85. Mozambique
86. Myanmar
87. Nambia
88. Nepal
89. Netherlands
90. Nicaragua
91. Niger
92. Nigeria
93. Pakistan
94. Panama
95. Paraguay
96. Peru
97. Philippines
98. Poland
99. Portugal
100. Republic of Korea
101. Republic of Moldova
102. Romania
103. Russian Federation
104. Rwanda
105. San Marino
106. Sao Tome and Principe
107. Senegal
108. Seychelles
109. Sierra Leone
110. Slovakia
111. Solvenia
112. South Africa
113. Spain
114. Sri Lanka
115. Sudan
116. Switzerland

117. Syrian Arab Republic
118. Thailand
119. The former Yugoslav Republic of Macedonia
120. Togo
121. Tunisia
122. Turkey
123. Turkmenistan
124. Uganda
125. Ukraine
126. United Republic of Tanzania
127. Uruguay
128. Uzbekistan
129. Venezuela
130. Vietnam
131. Yemen
132. Zambia
133. Zimbabwe

ASSOCIATE MEMBERS

1. Aruba
2. Flanders
3. Macau
4. Madeira
5. Netherlands Antilles

Permanent Observer of the World Tourism Organisation

Holy See

APPENDIX-V

World Tourism Organisation (WTO)

SOME IMPORTANT DECLARATIONS

***COURTESY* : WTO**

Recife Charter on Senior Tourism

1. As conventional mass tourism has matured so has the generation of actual and potential leisure travellers worldwide. At the same time, tourism is seeking new horizons and products. Therefore, the growing number and unprecedented proportion of senior citizens in the world represent immediate challenges and multiple development opportunities for the tourism sector in Latin American countries. Moreover, tourism is a viable way of pursuing and maintaining the quality of life of seniors.

2. In targeting seniors as leisure travellers, the public sector and the tourism industry alike should consider quality of life of seniors, such as psychological well-being, personal fulfilment and health. At the same time, they should work to ensure fair and democratic access to tourism regardless of socio-economic level.

3. Senior tourism should be viewed as integral part of mainstream tourism, not as a segregated group, because it shares the same networks and establishments with other users and consumers. Because it is so diverse, it requires imaginative and appropriate marketing and distribution wherein tourism products are designed to meet the needs and characteristics of the various sectors. The importance of senior tourism resides in the fact that it is less a special market but rather more a foreshadowing of future mass tourism.

4. To ensure the quality of tourism experience for seniors, tourism planners and organizers should provide for :

(1) basic quality factors, such as safety and security, sanitation and health, environmental considerations, independence, accessibility to services and facilities and consumer protection standards;

(2) interaction with the people and places visited;

(3) educational and cultural experiences;

(4) entertainment and outdoor activities;

(5) facilities for social activities; and

(6) appropriate pacing and format of tourism leisure activities.

5. In establishing tourism security programs, decision-makers and planners should employ program based on model solutions and tourism policy guidelines derived from the experience of organizations, destinations and countries, and from publications such as those available through the World Tourism Organization. For example, Latin America may wish to consider the experience of the United States and Europe in meeting the security needs of seniors.

6. Sanitation in tourist sites and establishments is important due to its role in the health of senior visitors and in seniors' perception of the respect displayed towards them. To provide for a quality tourism product for seniors, tourism developers need to protect the natural and beautiful, provide open spaces and reduce density, restore the historical, value local culture and traditions, and design low-horizon structures in harmony with the natural environment, while gaining community acceptance.

7. Decision-makers and planners should gain an understanding of the aging process and universal design concepts for the creation of literature, graphics, and facilities. Special attention should be given to designing and upgrading tourism facilities without architectural and interior design barriers to maximize comfort of users and to anticipate temprorary or permanent disabilities. These considerations should be standard in the conception of all new tourism projects and the facilities' renovation. The facilities used by seniors should also feature ergonomic furniture and fittings, sufficient lighting, and signage easy to follow and understand. Travel literature and collateral materials, such as menus, bills, and instructions, should be easy to read and understand. Oral communication should be clear and intelligible. Guidelines and resources are available from such sources as the American Association of Retired Persons.

8. In response to senior consumer rights, the travel industry including promotional authorities, providers, facilities, and destinations should ensure complete, honest, and accurate communications about products, services and pricing. This information should be complemented by opportunities to inquire fully into advertised products, useful advice on

travel health and safety risks and responsiveness to questions, requests and complaints.

9. The tourism industry is encouraged to invest in the education and training of its staff to meet the needs of senior travellers with hospitality, courtesy, understanding, patience, nonrestricted activity options, good service and clear language, including foreign languages spoken by senior international visitors. A special effort is needed to prepare tour guides and the young tourism staff to understand and communicate with seniors. To this end cooperation between the industry and senior organizations is highly recommended.

10. In pursuing high quality standards of service for seniors, the tourism industry is encouraged to use modern total quality management techniques and methodologies; audit management, programs and services; and institute certification. This will also help to lower tourism industry costs and thus make tourism more accessible to seniors.

11. Senior tourism as part of mainstream tourism, today and tomorrow, plays an important role in the development and globalization of local, regional and world economies. Senior tourism, therefore, expects to benefit from the ongoing process of dismantling international and national barriers to trade and from the use of electronic technologies in the tourism sector. However, senior travel communities in Latin America and in Brazil in particular are concerned with the persistence of economic barriers to tourism, such as high air and hotel tariffs.

12. More contacts and negotiations between the senior travel community and the tourism industry are necessary to put in place advocacy groups to reduce price barriers to senior travel. It is hoped that, as a result, both parties will mutually benefit, particularly with regards to the senior tourism potential to use air transport and hotel capacity off-season in a sustained way. Consideration should also be given to the cooperative experience of the travel industry and senior communities in other regions, particularly in Europe and North America.

13. In targeting potential senior tourism demand for Latin America from other regions, it is important to take into consideration the different characteristics of the respective markets, such as Europe, Canada, the United States and Japan. Each market needs to be accessed in a different way. At the same time, the destinations will need to offer high quality products to compete effectively with other tourism destinations.

14. As the World Tourism Organization forecasts the number of international tourist arrivals at 702 million by the year 2000 and 1,018 million by 2010, Latin America should mobilize to capture a corresponding share of this market by developing its tourism potential to accommodate seniors.

15. A research agenda is imperative in studying senior tourism in relationship to sociology, geriabucs, culture and economic development. The tourism industry will benefit from this research in targeting markets and products. Regional and international organizations and alliances, such as NAFTA, MERCOSUR, the International Sociological Association, and the World Tourism Organization, have a responsibility to coordinate and support this research agenda.

16. Regions should seek to maximize opportunities for exchange of senior tourism flows to learn from each other. Latin America, and Brazil as the host country for the Second International Conference on Senior Tourism can offer their spirit, enthusiasm, and entertainment as a valuable contribution to the enrichment of cultural experience and human relations for all.

Recife, Pernambuco, Brazil **15 September, 1996**

Adopted by acclamation at the closing of the Second International Conference on Senior Tourism (Olinda/Recife, Brazil, 12-15 September 1996) organized by the Brazilian Institute for Tourism EMBRATUR and the Brazilian Association of Senior Age Clubs in cooperation with the State Government of Pernambuco, the World Tourism Organization (WTO) and the American Association of Retired Persons (AARP).

Bali Declaration on Tourism

Second International Forum
Bali, Indonesia, 24-27 September, 1996

THE SECOND INTERNATIONAL FORUM ON "PARLIAMENTS AND LOCAL AUTHORITIES: TOURISM POLICY-MAKERS";

HELD in Indonesia, from 24 to 27 September 1996, convened by the World Tourism Organization (WTO), in cooperation with the Government of Indonesia and with the support of the House of Representatives of this country, was opened by the Speaker of the House of Representatives of the Republic of Indonesia, and was attended by 465 delegates representing 72 countries comprising Members of Parliaments, local authorities, national tourism administrations and tourism industry;

HAVING DISCUSSED tourism development policies used by all countries to raise the well-being of their respective societies in a way that encompasses the physical, spiritual and intellectual dimensions, while protecting and preserving the environment as well as social and cultural values so that sustainable tourism development prevails;

RECOGNIZING

That tourism can promote the well-being of societies, especially that of local communities, and expand employment and business opportunities by keeping abreast of scientific and technological progress, which has the capacity to make a significant contribution to the future development of tourism;

That tourism, which is now enjoyed by all social strata, has become an important human need and is no longer just a leisure activity;

That tourism is a major contributor to the world economy, which has grown to the point where it can exert an influence upon every aspect of human life;

That tourism can really enhance the quality of human relationships, regardless of ethnic, racial, religious or socio-cultural differences and has a great role to play not only in promoting mutual understanding and better relations among nations but also in helping to bring about world peace;

That tourism is based on the diversity of nature, religions, cultural values and traditions and it can have both negative and positive influences, so balanced relationships between people and their natural and cultural environment need to be preserved and national identity invigorated;

That tourism development requires parliaments and governments to formulate and implement policies and regulations flexibly by involving interested groups and local communities;

REFERRING to the Manila Declaration adopted in 1980 under the auspices of WTO,

AGREES, in an effort to have an appropriate basis for formulating tourism policy, to declare the following :

1. Tourism development is to be aimed at the well-being of local communities, the promotion of mutual understanding to achieve peace, the conservation of nature and the environment, and the preservation of traditions as well as diverse social, cultural and religious values;
2. Tourism development in tourist destination areas must be able to maintain a balance between the interests of local communities and those of tourists; tourism development is to promote a tolerant attitude between tourists and local communities based on the principle of equality so that mutual understanding and respect for differences are enhanced, and a safe, peaceful and calm atmosphere prevails. In this context, all forms of organized sex tourism, especially the sexual exploitation of children, must be banned and fought;

3. Tourism development is to be carried out on the basis of careful planning with the broad involvement and active participation of local communities, including women and the young generation, and the private sector to balance economic, social, cultural and religious values and environmental conservation so that sustainable development is achieved;
4. Tourism development is to be implemented in a way that not only increases revenues at state and local levels, but also improves the quality of life at community level by expanding business opportunities and increasing employment and capitalizing to the optimum on scientific and technological progress, while preventing any negative impact that may emerge;
5. Tourism development is to involve governments, both the central and local levels, the private sector, the community and the media in a harmonious and balanced way;
6. Tourism development requires parliaments, as representative institutions of the people, to play a significant role in formulating tourism policy and supervising its implementation, not only at the local and national levels but also internationally;
7. Implementation of tourism policy should be carried out in a way that strikes a good balance between a wide decentralization and coordination at the national level;
8. Tourism development must be able to build economic links that bridge the gap between developed and developing countries by enhancing cooperation in infrastructure development, human resources, promotion and marketing;
9. Tourism development requires parliaments, governments and local authorities to promote all initiatives that can help to make society more attentive to tourism, a phenomenon that has been, and will be in the coming years, a fundamental factor of economic growth, regional development and job creation, as well as of peace and prosperity;
10. The adoption of such policies requires a continued close cooperation and partnership between the various public administrations and between these and the private sector.

Malta Declaration

Adopted at the International Conference on 'Marketing the Mediterranean as a Region'
(Sliema, Malta, 9 November, 1996)

In pursuit of the decisions taken at the Hyeres les Palmiers (France) and Casablanca (Morocco) Conferences, the Malta Conference proposes to draw up an Action Plan :

(1) To explore the feasibility, with an independent group of experts, of a regional brand image, which will guarantee an authentic Mediterranean identity;

(2) To set up, under WTO auspices, a Centre, which, with the co-ordination of representatives of Mediterranean states, local authorities, industry associations and the private sector, would facilitate the promotion of :

- human resources development in the industry, including training,
- appropriate studies, through a Mediterranean tourism data base;
- the improvement of intra-Mediterranean surface and air communications;
- the formulation of a marketing campaign to highlight and promote the uniqueness of the mediterranean;
- the dissemination of tourism information to the general and professional media; and
- the organization of sectoral workshops for private and public bodies active in tourism, thus facilitating the eventual implementation of the Action Plan.

The Centre will liaise with EMTO and MEMTTA through appropriate links, seeking to strengthen sub-regional activities.

The budget of this Centre will be covered by other activities it will generate, as well as funding by other agencies.

The Conference welcomed the offer by the Maltese Minister for Tourism to host the Centre in Malta and fund its operations for the first year.

Male′ Declaration on Sustainable Tourism Development

Adopted at the Asia-Pacific Ministers' Conference on Tourism and Environment

(Male′, Maldives, 16th February, 1997)

WHEREAS the Asia-Pacific Tourism Ministers' Conference on Tourism and Environment was held on 16th February 1997, in Male′, Republic of Maldives, convened by the World Tourism Organization with the participation of delegations of 25 States, Affiliate Members, international organizations, regional organizations and observers, to clarify and define the linkage between tourism and environment, as well as to consider the responsibility of States and the private sector for achieving a high degree of sustainable tourism development;

WHEREAS the theme of the conference, "Tourism 2000—Building a Sustainable Future for Asia-Pacific", attests to the unanimous sentiment on the part of the conference participants that tourism can and should promote environmental health and integrity, and that the substantial and ongoing investment of financial, human, and natural resources in tourism development requires a fiduciary responsibility to the sustainability and continued viability of the industry for the benefit of communities and nations; and

WHEREAS there is recognition and appreciation for the uniqueness and diversity of natural environments, peoples, cultures, and heritages of the Asia-Pacific countries and their importance for tourism's potential for cross-cultural learning, international understanding, and world peace; and

WHEREAS the conference participants have explored the many policy-related and technical issues involved in sustainability, with an emphasis on those of particular relevance to the public sector; now, therefore,

BE IT RESOLVED by conference that the participants of the Asia-Pacific Ministers' Conference on Tourism and Environment agree in principle to:

Pledge continuing support for the vision and goals of a sustainable future, as conceived and articulated in the 1987 Brundtland Commission report, the 1992 Earth Summit, the Rio Declaration, and Agenda 21, and further extended to the tourism industry through subsequent efforts such as Agenda 21 for the Travel and Tourism Industry, the World Conference on Sustainable Tourism, and the 1996 International Conference on Tourism and Heritage Management, encompassing the following precepts:

- Fostering awareness of environmental ethics in tourism among communities and consumers;
- Conservation and sustainable use of resources;
- Public guardianship of the natural environment;
- Reducing consumption and waste;
- Natural, social and cultural diversity;
- Integrated tourism planning for sustainability;
- Support for local economies;
- Local community involvement;
- Consulting tourism stakeholders and the public;
- Human resource development;
- Responsible tourism marketing;
- Ongoing inquiry into sustainability issues;
- Measurements to monitor tourism's impacts on environment, culture and heritage; and
- Use of environmental impact assessments in tourism planning.

Commit resources to environmental protection and to improving the quality and professionalism of our human resources to create a valuable and meaningful visitor experience and to meet the needs of a competitive global environment,

Emphasize the urgency of sustainability for the health of both the tourism industry and the world economy, and especially for vulnerable ecosystems such as small island states;

Intensify efforts to make operational those policies and practices that promote sustainability, including further refinement of sustainable indicators to measure progress, realizing that research and technological advances have brought us to the point where sustainable action can now proceed;

Strive to provide the leadership, training, and technical support needed by communities to enable them to become fully aware of, and involved with, the processes by which tourism is planned and developed;

Support an active and prominent role for governments at all levels—national, provincial and local—in planning and promoting sustainable development;

Seek greater international and regional cooperation among Asian-Pacific nations in collaborating on sustainable tourism programs and sharing resources, expertise and information on best practices and experiences;

Call on the WTO and other appropriate bodies to expand the base of knowledge on sustainability issues, problems, and solutions for achieving sustainable balance;

Strengthen and promote cooperation with the many tourism-related businesses and organizations that comprise the private and non-governmental sectors, in recognition of the costs and effort that sustainability requires for optimizing opportunities; and

BE IT FINALLY RESOLVED that the participants urge their governments to use the principles of this Declaration as a policy tool to measure progress towards sustainability and to assist in the implementation of sustainable practices.

Manila Declaration on the Social Impact of Tourism

WE, the representatives of governments and private groups from 77 countries and territories, gathered for the World Tourism Leaders' Meeting on the Social Impact of Tourism, under the joint auspices of the World Tourism Organization (WTO) and the Government of the Republic of the Philippines,

HAVING DISCUSSED the social impact of tourism and considered how to maximize their positive aspects and minimize their negative effects,

BELIEVING that tourism will continue to generate substantial economic and social benefits for communities and countries and that it is not the sole cause of social problems attributed to or associated with it,

BEING DETERMINED to remove the social abuses and exploitation arising from, associated with or occasioned by tourism and its related activities,

HEREBY COMMIT OURSERVES TO:

1. Support greater involvement of communities in the planning, implementation, monitoring and evaluation processes of tourism policies, programs and projects within the context of national objectives and priorities, and for this purpose introduce community awareness campaigns to inform people of the benefits to be gained from tourism development;

2. Improve people's standard ofliving through tourism by providing economic and social opportunities for wider participation and, wherever possible and acceptable, dispersal of tourism activities and destinations to outlying areas to increase rural incomes;
3. Ensure that tourism development planning preserve the legacy, heritage and integrity of tourism destinations worldwide and respect the social and cultural norms of society, particularly among the indigenous communities, and to this end, control the rate of growth of the tourism sector where it may jeopardize local communities and social values;
4. Cooperate with and encourage the business community engaged in tourism and the travel trade to create the right image and develop appropriate marketing tools for the destination countries, and to undertake education, information and communication services to sensitize visitors to the culture and behavioural expectations of host communities;
5. Recognize the role of human resources development in tourism and establish long-term programmes that support greater employment of the local labour force in tourism and provide appropriate measures as well as opportunities for a greater and more positive participation of women and youth;
6. Enhance and strengthen international coordination and monitoring systems through liaison and networking among governments, private sector and concerned parties with a view to promoting the positive aspects and eradicating the negative impacts of tourism;
7. Further mobilize local and international support to prevent and control tourism-related abuse and exploitation of people, particularly women and children and other disadvantaged groups;
8. Encourage governments to promulgate and enforce legal regimes, both in the domestic and multilateral arenas, in order to eliminate undesirable social consequences of tourism through, among others, agreements that deprive malefactors of any safe haven anywhere;
9. Take into account the importance of tourism in the context of Agenda 21, for tourism is a major source of development but like other sectors, it uses resources and generates wastes and in the

process creates not only social and cultural but also environmental costs and benefits, of which the effects on biodiversity and fragile eco-systems like coral reefs, archaeological sites, mountains, coastal areas and wetlands constitute a particular concern and pose the imperative of having the world celebrate and, more importantly, observe the tenets of eco-tourism; and

10. Work towards the formulation and eventual adoption of a Global Code of Ethics for Tourism.

ADOPTED in Manila, Philippines on 22 May 1997

Montreal Declaration

Towards a Human and Social Vision of Tourism

PREAMBLE

(1) High ideals in the face of discrimination and the challenge of integration. Articles 1 and 2

(2) Social tourism: its strengths for the future:

to shape society. Articles 3 and 4

to promote economic growth. Articles 5, 6 and 7

to participate in the land management debate. Articles 8, 9 and 10

to partner in global development programmes. Articles 11 and 12

(3) Criteria for a definition of social tourism. Articles 13, 14 and 15

Conclusions

What does social tourism mean today? How do the key players in social tourism perceive their role? What are their beliefs and ambitions?

In the world today, what are the issues and the prospects facing us on the threshold of the third millennium?

Twenty-five years ago, in the Vienna Charter, BITS already set out the social, cultural, political and economic dimensions of tourism—a statement of fundamental significance for our time.

In turn, the World Tourism Organization, in its Manila Declaration, formally confirmed the objectives of social tourism.

What will social tourism mean in the years to come? This is the crucial issue to be addressed in the Montreal Declaration.

(1) SOCIAL TOURISM : a high ideal in the face of discrimination and the challenge of integration.

Today in a world

— in which growth in the wealthiest countries is spasmodic, and whole sections of the population suffer increasing deprivation, resulting in serious social unrest,

— in which advances in science and information technologies go hand in hand with a reduced workforce, opening up as yet undreamed of social and cultural opportunities,

—in which large economic alliances are formed, operating according to their own free-market logic,

— in which some countries experience rapid growth, opening up to the possibility of domestic tourism,

—in which other countries, and even whole continents, are trapped in appalling poverty,

—in which the right to a search for meaning is claimed everywhere,

... in this world, tourism is growing rapidly. We are witnessing spectacular increase in business and leisure travel, the opening-up of borders, the diversification of destinations, and new means of communication and transport.

Parallel to a global breakdown in the division between time devoted to work and time for leisure and travel, we are witness, in certain countries, to unacceptable forms of exploitation of local inhabitants, as extreme as the prostitution of children.

Art. 1. The Universal Declaration of Human Rights states that all human beings have the right to rest, leisure time, a limit to working hours, and to paid holidays.

This right is far from being universally accepted, the subjugation of leisure and tourism to the service of human needs must be vehemently pursued along the trail already blazed by social tourism, whose primary goal has always been access to travel and leisure opportunities for all.

Art. 2. The prime objective of all tourism development initiatives should be the full realization of each individual's potential, both as a person and as a citizen.

(2) SOCIAL TOURISM: ADVANTAGES FOR TOMORROW

Social tourism: "a shaper of society"

Art. 3. The aim of making tourist leisure accessible to all—including families, youth and elders—necessarily means being involved in the struggle against inequality and the exclusion of the culturally different, those of limited means or abilities, or those who live in developing countries.

To this end, specific measures need to be identified and implemented: the definition of social policies of tourism, the creation of infrastructures, the setting-up of support systems for the disadvantaged, awareness-raising and other staff training, etc. Modest initiatives, forming part of an overall strategy, can often be more effective 'shapers of society' than large-scale projects.

Art. 4. Holidays and travel can provide particularly apt occasions for personal enrichment, through the discovery of new places, cultures and civilizations, through physical, artistic, sport and leisure activities, by meeting people across educational or generation divides, and by other responsibilities taken on freely by tourists.

Social tourism operators wish to contribute to the improvement of human relationships, both through their training and their animation activities; social tourism is a vehicle for social cohesion.

Social Tourism: a promoter of economic growth

Art. 5. Hundreds of millions of people around the world travel and are welcomed by social tourism, which appeals to all income and age groups.

Social tourism flourishes in an economic climate informed by solidarity and social policy. In turn, social tourism offers, and will continue to do so to an increasing degree, an exceptional economic opportunity.

Tourism for all is a key to economic strength. It generates a continuous flow of people and investment, which contributes to regional development, produces national and international wealth, and stimulates the transfer of resources from the richer economies to the poorer countries.

Art. 6. Tourism must benefit the whole community. Its benefits must contribute to the social and economic development of regions and citizens as a whole. The tourism sector should both provide employment and guarantee the fundamental rights of all employees.

Art. 7. All the key players in the development of tourism are subject to the same economic constraints. Whether as entrepreneurs, facility managers, tour organizers or guides, educators or entertainers, are all economic agents, subject to the same expectations of competence, professionalism and performance.

The pursuit of a social development objective depends on exemplary management and improving results.

Social tourism participation in the land management practices

Art. 8. Long before its promotion by international organizations, the concept of 'sustainable development' had been adopted by social tourism and expressed in the following aims:

- reconcile tourism development, environmental protection and a respect for the identity of local communities;
- bring fresh resources into neglected regions;
- promote development without depletion of resources;
- generate local economic, social and cultural benefits.

While tourism is, on a global scale, one of the engines for regional development, it should never lead to the uncontrolled invasion of an area, the exploitation of the local population, or the destruction of its culture.

Art. 9. Tourism can, and should, represent hope for many fragile economies. The protection of the natural environment has to withstand acquisitive pressure from organizations or individuals intent on commercial or personal gain.

Art. 10. Social tourism, as entrepreneur and manager of tourist development projects, plays a key role with regard to tourists. Its duty is to raise awareness, inform and to inclucate respect for the environment and local communities.

Social tourism: a partner in global development programmes

Art. 11. The Stockholm Conference on Population and the Environment, the United Nations programmes and the Rio Earth Summit, among others, have clearly identified the responsibilities of present generations in setting limits to growth.

Tourism, when it is controlled and when it respects the natural environment and local communities, constitutes one of the economic, social and cultural hopes of many developing regions. For this reason, present and future social tourism operators are, and will be, well-placed to devise development projects, put in place legal and financial frameworks, and contribute to the management, training programmes and animation of all tourist projects planned for global development programmes.

Art. 12. Throughout the world, new forms of cooperation and partnership are, and will be, essential, since tourist development requires the support of many local authorities, social organizations, trade unions, financial partners, family, youth, cultural, sport, and ecology movements, and, of course, professionals in the tourist industry, among which, social tourism operators serving the public good.

(3) CRITERIA FOR A DEFINITION OF SOCIAL TOURISM

Art. 13. Any tourist organization (association, cooperative, mutal society, foundation, federation, not-for-profit organization, company, etc.) which, by its articles of association or statement of aims clearly identifies with social objectives and the aim of making travel and tourism accessible to the greatest number— thereby differentiating itself from the sole aim of profit maximization—may claim membership of the social tourism movement.

The word 'social' may evoke an increased sense of solidarity and fraternity, and be a source of hope for those many people in the world today who still have no leisure time.

Art. 14. The validity of this claim is subject to the following verifiable conditions:

1. The proposed activities bring together social, educational and cultural objectives favouring the respect and the development of the individual.
2. The target public is clearly identified, without discrimination on racial, cultural, religious, political, philosophical or social grounds.
3. A non-economic added-value forms an integral part of the proposed product.
4. A will to non-disruptive integration into the local environment is clearly expressed.

5. The type of activity and the price are clearly indicated in the contract documents. Prices are compatible with the stated social objectives. Annual surpluses, in whole or in part, will be re-invested for the improvement of services offered to the public.
6. Personnel management is in accordance with social legislation, and undertakes to promote job satisfaction and deliver appropriate on-going staff development training.

Art. 15. Tourism operators cannot look for justification to statutes or procedures, but rather to their actions in pursuit of a clearly stated objective.

Statutes vary indeed according to customs, practice and evolving legislation. It is only a means to an end. There in no single model in the world today.

Whatever the acknowledged achievements and successes, a significant and lasting social tourism cannot exist without the formulation and long-term maintenance of truly socially-minded policies for tourism at the regional, national and international level.

Those involved in social tourism intend to actively participate in the formulation and implementation of such policies.

Faithful to its origins, and facing the realities of today and the challenges of tomorrow, BITS intends to focus all its efforts to promote a social and human vision of tourism-related development.

BITS calls on all those who share that same vision for the future of men and women everywhere to work together for the achievement of these aims.